JEWELS

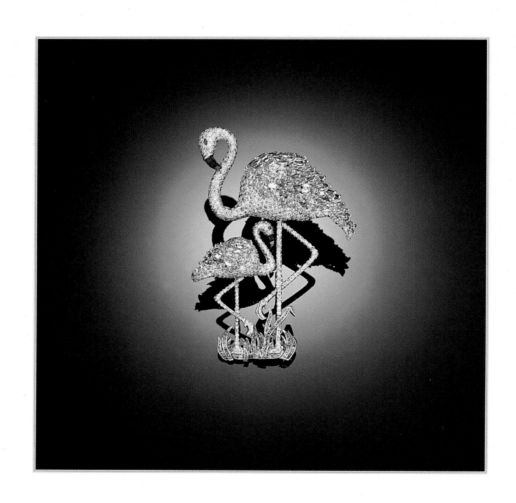

JEWELS

SUE HEADY

Grange
BOOKS

This edition published in 1999 by
An imprint of Grange Books PLC
The Grange, Kingsnorth Industrial Estate
Hoo, nr. Rochester, Kent
ME3 9ND

Produced by PRC Publishing Ltd,
Kiln House, 210 New Kings Road, London SW6 4NZ

1 84013 285 X

Printed and bound in China

JEWELS CONTENTS

A BRIEF HISTORY OF JEWELRY

Previous pages and Above: Lavishly set with precious stones, these pieces of Indian jewelry are typical of the Mughal Empire.

Right, top of page: A Victorian charm with a rose diamond edge.

Far Right: Victorian ruby and diamond cluster drop earrings and matching necklace.

BOTH MEN AND WOMEN HAVE WORN jewelry since ancient times, with different cultures developing different styles. Before man worked out how to carve stones and shape metal, jewelry was made from seeds, berries, shells and animal bones and teeth.

When man finally learnt how to manipulate metal, gold was the chosen medium. For example, some of the earliest pieces of jewelry to have been discovered are gold and date to 2,500BC, when the Sumerian civilization lived in southern Mesopotamia.

Slightly younger in age is the jewelry discovered in Tutankhamun's tomb, which dates to around 1327BC. Gold jewelry was very important in ancient Egypt, as it provided a splash of color to the white linen clothes that were worn at the time. It also played a very important part in funeral preparations, the dead—as in the case of Tutankhamun—being splendidly adorned. But it was not only the rich and royal; even the poor were buried with a simple gold necklace.

The Etruscans, whose Tuscan civilization was at its peak between 700 and 500BC, created some of the finest jewelry in ancient times. They are particularly known for mastering the difficult technique of granulation, which was used to create surface texture on gold.

The Hellenistic period (330–27BC) was rich in gold and jewelry, the distinctive feature of which was polychromy involving panels of colored stone or glass and enamel. Garnets, emeralds, amethysts and pearls were the stones used, many of them beautifully carved. It was the ancient Greeks who first developed intaglios (incised carving to be used as seals) and cameos (for purely decorative reasons).

Following on from the Greeks, the Romans developed the art of pierced work, by which a pattern was punched and cut through whichever metal was being used. It is interesting to see that before the start of the millennium, many of the major techniques involved in jewelry making had already been discovered.

Jewelry made in the Byzantine Empire incorporated all the techniques discovered in earlier years and added *cloisonné* enamel, which was to become one of the most distinctive features of the jewelry created during this era. Christian iconography pervaded Byzantine jewelry—pendant crosses were created and picture of saints and prophets were incorporated into various different pieces.

By the early 8th century, the pagan tradition of burying the dead adorned with jewelry had been abandoned in most parts of Europe, so very few pieces have survived from this time and it is, therefore, difficult to know exactly what was produced. However, documentary evidence proves that it continued to be an important feature of life.

In the Middle Ages, women, men and children wore jewelry—colored glass rather than gems being used to create copies for the young ones. Jewelry at this time served various purposes, some was decorative, some was functional and some was religious, and there were three distinct influences. Between 800 and the 13th century, the influence of the Byzantine Empire was apparent. At the end of the 13th century, Gothic style (reflecting the architecture of the time) was prevalent. And from the late 14th to late 15th century, jewelry became more refined and somehow softer, with an emphasis on natural ornamentation.

The voyages of discovery to the New World, which started with Christopher Columbus's

famous trip in 1492, brought many more gemstones, particularly Colombian emeralds, to Europe. As a result, more jewelry—of greater splendor—was made and worn during this Renaissance era. The intricate style and very high levels of craftsmanship were developed in Italy, before spreading west across Europe. The most famous Renaissance jeweler was the Italian Benvenuto Cellini (1500–71).

In the 1500s, court dress was very highly jeweled, with the men wearing all the gems in the first half of the century and the women taking the honors in the second half. Pendants were particularly popular, either attached to neckchains or attached to a lady's bodice or sleeve. As they were made to be seen from either side, both sides were decorated.

Renaissance rings were more heavily encrusted than ever before. Set with gemstones and cameos, they were worn in multiples on fingers and thumbs, and on different joints. In 1530, an inventory of Henry VIII's jewelry collection revealed that he had 234 rings.

Around 1700, there was a major innovation in the jewelry world as the emphasis shifted from the gold mount being dominant to the gemstones being of prime importance. As a result, gold settings receded into the background.

It was in the early 17th century that Paris emerged as Europe's style leader—both in the fashion and jewelry worlds, which would, from now on, remain irrevocably intertwined. For example, in the 1630s, flowing gowns with puffed sleeves and low necklines and softer hairstyles with shoulder-length ringlets were worn with pearls, which were regarded as gentler than gemset jewelry.

When Louis XV came of age in 1723, an elegant court style evolved in Paris and there was a definite trend away from cluster settings towards more flowing naturalism and ribbon bows—the most popular motif in Baroque jewelry. In the 1720s, the discovery of diamonds in Brazil saw a substantial increase in their use in jewelry designs.

In the 1730s, the Rococo style—characterized by asymmetry and jeweled feathers and flowers—was prevalent. In the 1760s, necklaces—either a simple row of pearls or a jeweled garland of intertwined ribbons and flowers—were being worn close to the neck. These often came with a matching pendant and a lower necklace known as an *esclavage*. Around this time, the first elements of neo-classical design started to seep into jewelry.

Throughout the 1700s, the division between day and evening wear became more distinct. Semi-precious stones, particularly garnets—started being used for pieces worn during the day—and the *chatelaine* developed as the most important piece of day jewelry for women. A *chatelaine* was an ornamental clasp that attached to a belt or girdle. Several chains hung from the clasp, at the end of which were useful household items such as keys, scissors and pincushions. Later, when *chatelaines* became fashionable pieces of jewelry, ornaments, rather than useful items, were attached to the clasp.

The French Revolution in 1789 resulted in a temporary decline in jewelry making. However, when Napoleon was made Emperor in 1804, the wearing of opulent jewelry came into fashion once again and the French jewelry houses increased their production. So essential were grand jewels that women who did not own their own parure would have to borrow a set from one of the jewelers for state occasions.

This state of affairs did not last long. In 1814, the Bourbons were restored to power, marking the start of a period of economic austerity. While men had been extravagantly adorned in previous years, wearing diamond buttons, rings and watches, their jewelry was now rather limited. Women, meanwhile, reverted to wearing semi-precious stones.

In the 1820s and 1830s, clashing semi-precious stones were all the rage. Twenty years later, major archaeological discoveries had a profound effect on jewelry design. The Revivalist era saw jewelry designers reproducing copies of the Etruscan and Greek styles that had been unearthed. The most influential jewelry maker at this time was the Italian Fortunato Pio Castellani (1793–1865), who established his house in 1814. Some of the Revivalist "copies" were so accurate that they were hard to distinguish them from the originals.

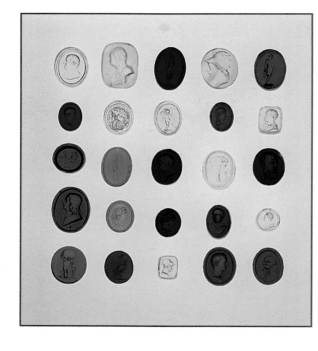

Above: Before faceting became widely used it was common for gems to be carved, the resulting stones could be used as seals as well as for purely decorative purposes. Not all beautiful jewelry is made from precious stones however; these superb intaglios are fashioned from colored glass.

Above Right: (From left to right), an antique diamond flowerspray pendant mounted en *pampilles*; a selection of rings, pendants, necklaces and brooches; stylized strawberries of citrines and diamonds.

Above, Far Right: Part of a suite, this ruby and diamond necklace features a ruby that weighs 24.59 carats.

Nineteenth century jewelry design also borrowed from the lavishly illustrated books that were starting to be produced and Japanese designs, such as cranes, bamboo and chrysanthemums, which were on show for the first time at the 1862 London Exhibition.

The *Belle Époque* era, which—translated from the French means "Fine Period"—refers to a time of settled and comfortable living that lasted from the end of the 19th century up until the outbreak of the First World War. During the era, there were three discernible divisions in jewelry design.

The first was the formal court jewelry, which was not unlike the pieces produced during the reign of Louis XVI and the First Empire. Certainly Edwardian design was influenced by the jewelry of the late 18th century, particularly that of Marie Antoinette. As a result, it featured garlands, wreaths, bows, tassels or a combination of all these elements. Almost all the fine jewelry at this time was "white." Recently discovered South African diamonds, the invention of cultured pearls in Japan and the use of platinum rather than gold, resulted in an overall look that was white.

The second was Art Nouveau jewelry, which dominated the 1890s and early 1900s. Named after Siegfried Bing's avant-garde interior decoration shop called the "Maison de l'Art Nouveau," which opened in Paris in 1896, the term was applied to all the decorative arts, including jewelry. Its main features were free flowing, swirling lines with asymmetrical motifs representing a romanticized nature. Intertwining flowers, butterflies, dragonflies and ethereal female faces were created with colored stones and very sophisticated enamel work, particularly incorporating the difficult but effective *plique-a-jour* method.

René Lalique, the leading French exponent of Art Nouveau jewelry, was known for his originality and his exquisite craftsmanship. From the age of 16, he was apprenticed to the Parisian silversmith and jeweler, Louis Aucoq, and he later produced pieces for both Cartier and Boucheron. His own work was so well received at the 1900 Paris Exhibition, that his jewelry immediately became very popular among the royal families and aristocracy of Europe.

The third was the slightly less important Arts and Crafts movement in England, which was heavily promoted by Liberty's. Common features were hand-beaten metal surfaces, soft colored cabochon stones and enamels.

By 1910, jewelry was already starting to exhibit the linear approach that would be championed during the Art Deco era. With its stylized designs and geometric patterns, Art Deco was a direct challenge to the floral, free-flowing work of the earlier Art Nouveau era. It was officially launched in Paris in 1925 through the Exposition Internationale des Art Decoratifs, which gave the movement its name.

The Art Deco movement was influenced by the geometry and abstraction of Cubist painting, the linear forms of the Vienna Secession, Diaghilev's *Ballets Russes* (which was performed in Paris from 1909) and the discovery of Tutankhamun's tomb in 1922. In addition, imitations of Indian Mughal jewelry—strings of beads or a large carved pendant—played their part. Pieces produced by Cartier dominated the era.

In the 1930s, accessories, such as the frame of an evening bag, cigarette holders and powder compacts, became an essential part of women's jewelry. It was at this time that Van Cleef & Arpels created

GEMSTONES

DIAMONDS

RUBIES

the *minaudière*, a vanity case with special compartments for lipstick, powder, rouge, a watch, cigarettes and a lighter.

Costume jewelry hit new heights in the late 1920s and 1930s, encouraged by Coco Chanel and Elsa Schiaparelli, who believe even well-heeled ladies who could afford the real thing should invest in the more imaginative and exciting fake pieces. The most highly regarded creator of costume jewelry was the Italian Fulco Santostefano della Cerda, Duke of Verdura, who worked for Chanel before setting up his own company.

With the outbreak of the Second World War, jewelry production stopped. When it restarted in the 1950s, the theme was light-hearted. Large necklaces, set with semi-precious stones, complemented Dior's famous "New Look": a low neckline, narrow waist and full skirt. It was at this time that bib necklaces were first made.

Since 1960, the jewelry world has undergone dramatic change. While the major houses—Cartier, Van Cleef & Arpels, Bulgari—continue to create stunning pieces of classic jewelry, many individual designers have sprung up and started producing innovative modern jewelry. They use any kind of material, manipulated into any kind of shape: there is no set style as there was in previous years.

The word diamond comes from the Greek *adamas* meaning invincible. Diamond, a form of crystallized carbon, is the hardest substance found in nature and is the most well-known stone to man.

Up until the first quarter of the 18th century, all diamonds came from India and Borneo. In 1725, diamonds were found in Brazil, but still had to be imported into Europe via Goa and sold as Oriental gems, as many Europeans did not believe Brazilian diamonds to be real. The Brazilian deposits were exhausted by 1875, but—luckily—diamonds had been discovered nine years earlier in South Africa, which immediately became the world's largest producer. Now, it is fifth in the world behind Russia, Botswana, Zaire and Australia, which is currently the largest producer.

Ask any number of people how they would describe a diamond and the majority of the responses would be along the lines of: "A very hard, white and very expensive precious stone." The truth is that although many diamonds are white, they are found in several different colors and it is the "fancy" diamonds (as they are known) that are the most prized. This is primarily because only one in every 100,000 or so has a deep enough color to qualify as a fancy colored stone.

"Fancy" diamonds vary in color from yellow to red to blue. Yellow, orange and brown are the most common. They are, therefore, less expensive than the most prized, which are red, green and blue. Reasons for the coloration of diamonds include the presence of boron (blue), the presence of nitrogen (yellow), a deformed chemical structure (brown, pin and mauve) and natural radiation (green).

The word ruby comes from the Greek *ruber*, meaning red. Formed from aluminium oxide, rubies are red-colored corundums. After diamonds, they are the most valuable gems in the world.

Until the 16th century, a ruby was called a carbuncle, along with all the world's other red stones: a *balas* ruby was actually a red spinel, a Brazilian ruby was really a topaz and a Bohemian ruby was what we now know as a garnet. The Oriental ruby was the only red corundum and, therefore, the only real ruby. The adjective "Oriental" indicates the ruby's traditional sources: Burma, Thailand, India and Sri Lanka, which are all still important today. Deposits have also been found in Vietnam, Afghanistan and Tanzania.

In general, a ruby over ten carats that has not undergone heat treatment is rare and those over 35 carats in their natural, unheated form are virtually unheard of. In fact, to say that rubies of this size are fit for a king would be no exaggeration, because, until the middle of the 19th century, only the sovereign of Burma, or an individual deemed worthy by him, would have been allowed the privilege of possessing such a gemstone.

If a ruby is sold with a gemmologist's certificate of origin, the desirability and value of the stone are greatly increased. Even more so if the certificate also states that the stone has not been subject to heat treatment. The latter is important, because more and more gems are being heat treated to enhance their appearance and thus their value. Heat treating involves cooking in a furnace to intensify the gem's color and burn away inclusions. Heat treatment is very difficult for an expert to detect. As a result, treated stones are accepted commercially, but there will always be a demand for—and a higher price on—natural rubies.

DIAMONDS

Top: An Indian gem-set and enamel fringe necklace.

Above: The finest emeralds are a deep, rich grass green.

Far Right: An attractive Art Deco ruby and diamond necklace with diamond earrings. These pieces were made around 1925.

EMERALDS

Emerald comes from the Greek word *smaragdos*. Like aquamarines, they are a form of beryl. Rather like ruby, the word emerald was used to describe all green stones up until the late 19th century.

In ancient times, emeralds were only found in Upper Egypt, where the mines are now exhausted. Emeralds from the New World began to arrive in Europe soon after Christopher Columbus made his historic trip across the Atlantic Ocean in 1492. The first emeralds were pillaged from tombs, with in situ deposits not being found until 1537 in Colombia. Like diamonds, they had to be shipped through Goa and sold as Oriental gems in order to obtain the price of an emerald for them. Today, emeralds are found in South Africa, Zimbabwe, Zambia, Pakistan, Russia and Brazil.

Like other precious stones, where an emerald is mined is most important. Some of the most sought after emeralds in the world come from Colombia, in particular the mines of Muzo and Chivor. However, some of the world's most important emeralds are set in 16th century Indian jewelry. Originally thought to be mined in India, it is now known that they were taken to India from Colombia, for re-exporting to Europe. These emeralds are of better quality than those mined today, the best mines having been exhausted many years ago.

In the same way that rubies can only be red, emeralds are only ever green in color. However, the green may be different shades in different stones. Muzo emeralds, for instance, are a rich, deep grass green, with a slight yellow tinge and, simultaneously, a flash of blue. Lesser quality emeralds are paler and lack depth or brilliance.

SAPPHIRES

The word sapphire comes from the Greek *sappheiros* meaning blue. It refers to all corundums (aluminium oxides) that are not red (these are known as rubies). For, like diamonds, it is a common misconception that all sapphires are blue. "Fancy" sapphires can be yellow, green, brown, purple or pink, according to the presence of various types of mineral. The presence of chromium results in a pink sapphire, vanadium causes violet stones and iron produces either yellow or green sapphires.

In the 16th century, sapphires were not as highly regarded as other gems—their worth was less than half that of an emerald and four times less than a ruby of a similar weight. Up to the 19th century, sapphires came mainly from Burma and Sri Lanka. In 1870, deposits were also found in Thailand and Australia. Eleven years later, sapphires were discovered in Kashmir, where the most exceptional examples have been unearthed in modern times.

Indian sapphires from Kashmir are highly sought after because of their magnificent cornflower blue color, which tends—unlike the hue of other sapphires—to keep its character in the artificial light that fantastic gems are usually worn under at night. Sri Lankan sapphires, which are the most common, tend to be clearer and brighter than Indian and Burmese sapphires, but do not display the same strength of color.

Sapphires have been of great significance to past societies. For example, the Mystical Jews regarded the blue gemstones as a secret message from the beyond and the Persians thought the world rested on a giant sapphire, the sky being a reflection of the fabulous color of the stone.

PEARLS

The word pearl comes from the Latin *pirla*—a reference to the tear-shaped form of some pearls. A natural pearl is the only organic gemstone to be classed alongside precious gems. In fact, when they were first introduced into Europe from the Middle East, their value was determined to be greater than diamonds.

As a natural pearl is formed when an irritant or foreign body is present inside an oyster shell, so someone manually inserting an irritant into a shell can create a cultured pearl. Pearls that do not form a sphere are known as baroque (from the Portuguese barroco meaning irregular) pearls.

During the Renaissance, natural pearls came from the Persian Gulf, the Red Sea and the China Sea. In the 16th century, the Gulf of Mexico, the Caribbean and other regions nearby were also sources of pearls. These days, natural pearls are relatively rare, not only for environmental reasons, but also because cultured pearls are so common.

Cultured pearls have been produced in Japan at a commercial level since the end of the 19th century. Today, there are important pearl farms in Japan, Australia, China, Vietnam and the South Pacific Islands.

The two main criteria to consider when valuing pearls are color and luster. The most common pearls are white, while the most highly prized are pinkish rose pearls with a "fine orient" or luster. All good quality pearls are a perfect sphere and have a smooth, unblemished surface.

AMBER

Amber comes from the Arabic word *anbar* meaning to burn. Amber is the fossilized resin of an extinct pine tree that was submerged under the sea more than 30 million years ago. Essentially, it is an organic gem made of carbon compounds and a substance known as succinic acid.

It varies in color from pale yellow to reddish-brown and dark red/almost black, with the best quality amber being clear in nature. The most highly valued color has varied through history depending on fashion.

Since ancient times, it has been found washed up on the shores of the Baltic and in Burma. These days, it is also found in Central America, Lebanon, Canada and Alaska.

Turned into jewelry since ancient times, it was frequently used as a talisman (an object used to ward off evil spirits and bring good fortune to the wearer) and became popular during the Victorian era when it was used to make bead necklaces.

13

AMETHYSTS

Amethyst comes from the Greek word *amethustus*, meaning sober, because in ancient times it was supposed to stop wearers from becoming drunk.

In Renaissance times, amethysts were found in Russia, Ireland and what is now Germany, with smaller quantities discovered in India, Sri Lanka and Burma. Ever since the mid-19th century, however, the main source has been Brazil. The best quality amethysts come from Siberia.

Now semi-precious, amethysts (also known as purple quartz crystal) were once considered rare and, therefore, precious. As a result, they were mainly used for ecclesiastical or royal jewelry in the late 18th and early 19th centuries. Then, the discovery of large deposits of amethyst in Brazil in the 1850s sent prices plummeting.

Color (a deep, rich velvety purple) and clarity are indicators of a good quality amethyst.

CITRINES

Citrine, from the French *citron* meaning lemon, is a member of the quartz family and is, therefore, related to the amethyst. Usually yellow (hence its name), it can also be reddish-brown or reddish-orange.

Natural citrines—most of which are found in Brazil—are rare. Most stones sold as citrines are, in fact, smoky quartz or amethysts that have had their color changed by heat treatment.

During the 19th century, yellow citrines were used in copies of more expensive topaz jewelry. They continued to be popular right up until the Second World War, when it was difficult to get precious gemstones from the Far East. Cartier, for example, produced an interesting range of citrine jewelry.

CORAL

Coral, from the Greek *korallion*, is an organic gemstone made from the skeleton of the coral polyp, a small invertebrate marine animal.

The coral used for jewelry, known as *corallium nobile* (precious coral), was originally found in and around the Mediterranean, especially on the North African coast. Today, it is also found in Hawaii, Japan and Australia. The greater the depth at which the coral polyp lives, the paler the color of the coral. The colors that it is found in include shades of pink, black, white and red.

Coral has been a popular component of jewelry making since the Middle Ages, when it was worn in amulet form to protect the wearer from evil. In the first two-thirds of the 19th century, coral was very fashionable especially for daytime jewelry. Then the market became saturated and it fell from popularity. Coral enjoyed a brief revival in the Art Deco age and then again after the Second World War. Now, due to the effects of pollution, coral is hard to find, a fact reflected in rising prices.

GARNETS

Garnet derives from the Latin word *granatum*, meaning pomegranate. It is the name given to a family of semi-precious stones made from silicates. The best known are the almandine and pyrope, which tend to be a rich red, although almandines are sometimes purplish. Rarer grossulars can be yellowish brown or green.

Garnets came originally from India, Sri Lanka, what is now the Czech Republic and Russia. Today, they are mined in Brazil, Madagascar, Mozambique, the Czech Republic and India.

Very popular in the 18th century, almandines were used in the 19th century Renaissance Revival jewelry, as well as in formal parures. For although they are not particularly valuable in their own right, they can be very desirable when incorporated into a good piece of jewelry. They are still widely used, either faceted or *en cabochon*.

SPINELS

Spinels are made from magnesium aluminium oxide and are found in a wide variety of colors, including red, blue, violet and pink, in Burma and Sri Lanka.

Spinels are similar to rubies, and the untrained eye would probably have difficulty distinguishing between the two. To add to the confusion, spinel occurs with ruby in its natural form and was known as a *balas* ruby until the 19th century, when it was discovered that they were separate minerals. Prior to that, when ostentatious jewelry had needed larger stones, garnets and spinels had often been used.

One of the best known spinels is the so-called "Black Prince's ruby," which is the central stone in the Imperial State Crown, made in 1838 by Rundell Bridge and Rundell for the coronation of Queen Victoria.

TURQUOISE

Turquoise, from the French *pierre turquoise*, refers to the place—Turkey—where this stone was first thought to be found. In fact, Constantinople was only the trading center for turquoise, it was not the source. Traditionally, turquoise comes from the Sinai Peninsula and Iran. More recently, it has been found in Mexico.

Turquoise is a hydrous phosphate of copper and aluminium, which has been valued as a gem of thousands of years. It was particularly popular in the late 18th and early 19th centuries because of its fashionable bright, sky blue color and affordability.

The best turquoise is flawless and uniform in color, but as turquoise is highly porous, the stone in which it is found may leave markings on its surface and, once it has been set in jewelry, the acids from the wearer's skin may discolor it. Certainly this is why turquoise in antique jewelry often takes on a grayish green color.

OPALS

The word opal is from the Sanskrit *upala* meaning precious stone, but it is—of course—only a semi-precious stone. Not a true mineral, it is made from silica and water.

Known to the ancient Romans, who mined them in what is now Slovakia, opals are now found in Brazil, Mexico, the United States and Australia. The latter has been the largest producer in the world since deposits were found in the mid-19th century.

There are two main types of opal: common and precious. Common opals have a milky white sheen, while the precious ones are known for their iridescence, caused by tiny opal spheres that cause a play of colors as a result of diffraction of light. Precious opals, which tend to be virtually opaque, vary in color from deep blue to dark gray or black.

TOPAZ

Topaz comes from the Greek *topazos*, which means desert place—the gems originally came from the uninhabited St John's Island in the Red Sea. It is an aluminium silicate that occurs in several colors, including blue, pink, orange and yellow, the latter being the most common. Other sources include Central Europe, Sri Lanka, Burma and Brazil.

Topaz has been popular since the late 18th century and in the 19th century was highly prized, because of its brilliant color and lustrous clarity—light sherry brown is the most sought after color.

Above Left: Indian jewelry set with cultured pearls and turquoise.

Below: A diamond tiara in the garland style.

15

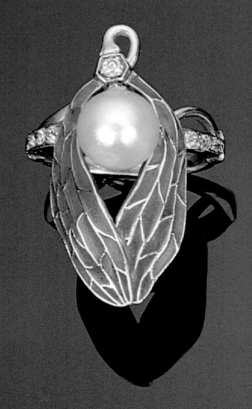

Previous pages: A collection of Art Nouveau rings. See pages 28–29.

AT ITS SIMPLEST, A RING IS A CIRCULAR band of material that is usually worn on a finger (or thumb), but can also be worn on a toe. Slightly more complex are rings set with gems, which consist of two parts: the circular band is known as the shank or hoop and the raised part on which the gemstone is set is called the bezel. Usually, they are made from gold, silver or platinum, but they can also be made from coral, turtle shell and jade, as well as plastic and cheap metals.

Since they were first introduced in the third millennium BC, both men and women have worn rings in Eastern and Western cultures. In the beginning, rings were not actually used as jewelry, but as money. And the easiest way to carry money (especially at a time when clothes did not have pockets) was on a finger or wrapped around a wrist.

When they were first worn for personal adornment, rather than practical reasons, only one ring was worn. However, from Roman times onward, several rings were worn, one of which was usually a guard ring, which was very simple in design and served to keep more valuable rings in place.

In the 16th century, a trend developed for wearing rings other than on the fingers. Women would sew them on to their dresses or string them to a piece of ribbon that they would hang around their neck.

Wedding rings were an invention of the 19th century. Engagement rings, more commonly known as betrothal rings, had been used since Roman times, but it was only in the 1800s that brides started receiving a wedding ring in addition to an engagement ring.

Originally, the bride wore her betrothal ring on the third finger on her left hand, because it was believed that there was a vein (*vena amoris*) running directly from that finger to the heart. Unlike today, the ring did not have to remain on the third finger—it could be worn wherever the wearer so desired. Today, bridegrooms the world over also wear wedding rings, along with their brides.

Other types of ring that have been produced for special occasions include mourning, keeper and sergeant rings. Mourning rings were worn in memory of a deceased person; keeper rings performed the same role as guard rings and sergeant rings were given by barristers to the sovereign, officials and friends when they were called to the position of Sergeant-at-Law.

Another group of rings are those that come under the heading of religious—they include devotional, ecclesiastical and papal rings. A devotional ring would have a sacred monogram or holy name imprinted on it; ecclesiastical rings were worn by ecclesiastical dignitaries, including abbots and bishops; and papal rings were probably given as souvenirs to pilgrims who visited the Vatican.

Then there are functional rings, such as signet and key finger rings. The former were used from early times to authenticate documents, while the latter had the ward of a key attached.

In addition, there are many other types of ring that do not necessarily have a specific function, but have their own individual name. These include cluster, crossover, eternity and snake rings, all of which are mentioned in this chapter.

GEMST NES

Above, Far Left: The best cut for a diamond is recognized to be a brilliant cut. A brilliant cut diamond has 58 facets (or surfaces), which minimize the amount of light that escapes through the bottom of the stone and thus increase the brilliance of the stone. The brilliant-cut diamond in this ring, which has a plain hoop, weighs 2.96 carats.

Cluster rings have been very popular ever since the mid-19th century. Here we have three excellent examples.

Above Left: This ring features a central brilliant-cut diamond, with a pear-shaped sapphire surround and diamond highlights.

Below Left: This example features a simple, cushion-shaped cluster of diamonds.

Above: An oval-shaped emerald and brilliant-cut diamond cluster ring, with diamond-set shoulders.

BRILLIANCE

DIAMOND

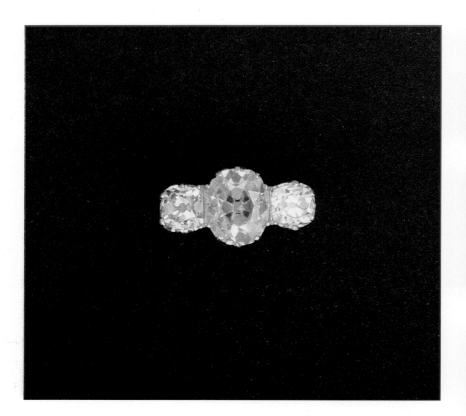

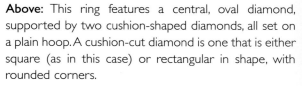

Above: This ring features a central, oval diamond, supported by two cushion-shaped diamonds, all set on a plain hoop. A cushion-cut diamond is one that is either square (as in this case) or rectangular in shape, with rounded corners.

Center Top: This is an unusual, brilliant-cut diamond nine-stone open-work panel ring.

Center Left: Note the carved soulders of this diamond marquise-shaped panel ring, which is set on a plain hoop.

Right, Top and Center: These two rings would undoubtedly make popular choices as engagement rings. The one at the top of the page a brilliant-cut diamond solitaire which was estimated at Christie's in London at £2,200-2,500, while the ring below it is a brilliant-cut diamond three-stone ring, which was estimated at £1,800-2,200.

Above: This ring has two brilliant-cut diamonds, surrounded by three cushion-shaped emeralds.

Far Left, Above and Below: These two rings offer a little bit more than the simple solitaire ring. The one above has four graduated baguette-cut diamonds on either side, while the other has four small stones on either side of a brilliant-cut diamond.

Left, Above and Below: These are very interesting rose-diamond rings, made around 1830. The *fleur-de-lis* setting represents the Bourbon emblem of a lily and it was thought that Charles X distributed these rings to members of the French nobility—at the instigation of his daughter-in-law the Duchesse de Berri who was the mother of Charles X's heir—in an attempt to gain support. As it was, the gesture failed. When Charles X abdicated in 1830, Louis Philippe of the House of Orleans was elected lieutenant-general of the kingdom and, after the Revolution, was given the title of "King of the French."

The ring above is slightly larger than the other, but they both had the same estimate at Christie's in London of £800-1,200.

ROSE DIAMOND

Above: This ring features a rectangular-cut, cut-cornered diamond weighing 6.97 carats, with two baguette-cut diamonds on T shoulders either side. An accompanying certificate from the British Gem Testing Laboratory states that the stone is Exceptional White + (D) Vs2, while an accompanying letter states that the gem is potentially flawless. Due to the superb quality of the diamond Christie's did not make an estimate, which means that the price they expected the ring to fetch would be very high indeed.

The ring was mounted by the famous jewelry house of Cartier, which was founded in Paris in 1847 by Louis-Francois Cartier and shortly thereafter started creating jewelry for various royal families around the world. It has continued to produce top class goods ever since.

Above: The 8.18 carat diamond in the center of this ring is surrounded by single, baguette-cut diamonds, all set on a plain hoop. It was sold with a certificate from the British Gem Testing Laboratory, which states that the stone is Rare White (G) VVs1.

There are four important factors to be considered when grading a diamond: cut, color, clarity and carat weight, the most important of which is color. The less color in a stone, the rarer it is. So the diamond in the ring on the left, which is graded "D," is the finest white stone, while "Z" would appear tinted. This stone, graded a "G" is pretty close to being colorless, hence the fairly high price of £40,000-50,000.

BAGUETTE

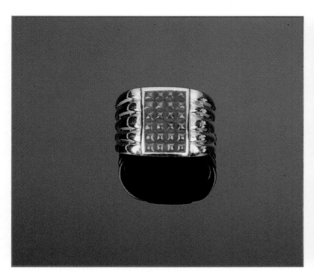 

Above, Left and Right: These two rings are very different in style, but both feature cabochon-cut gems. The main feature of the ruby ring above, with its graduated ribbed shoulders, is the pavé-set cabochon ruby rectangular panel. The ring on the right is simpler, and features a large cabochon sapphire in an unadorned setting.

The term cabochon comes from the French word for a doorknob, *caboche*, and refers to the smooth, rounded and highly polished surface of the gem. This type of cut was used hundreds of years ago, before the development of faceting (the cutting of a gemstone), and was only revived during the Art Nouveau era (1890s–early 1900s).

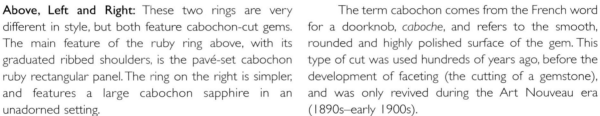

CABOCHON

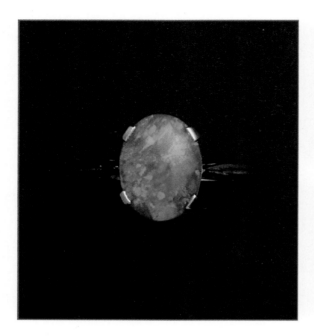

Above: The opal in this simple ring is black and, therefore, comes under the precious category.

Top and Above: Eternity rings, which date back 4,000 years, are typically made from one circular band, set with a continuous row of gemstones (usually diamonds) of the same size and cut, and are sometimes used as wedding rings.

In this regard, the two square-cut diamond eternity rings in the above picture are very traditional. More modern, is the eternity ring at the top with three bands that feature not only diamonds, but also sapphires and rubies.

In Elizabethan times, some eternity rings differed in that they were made in the shape of an encircling snake swallowing its tail.

Top: This is a square-cut emerald and diamond vertical line ring, with two baguette-cut diamonds either side.

Above: This brilliant-cut diamond single-stone ring has three diamonds on either side.

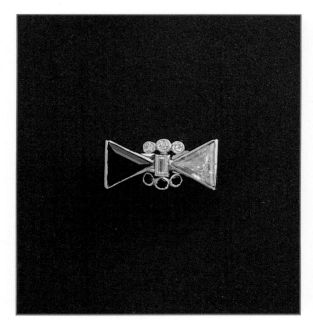

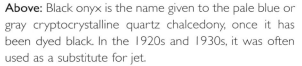

Above: Black onyx is the name given to the pale blue or gray cryptocrystalline quartz chalcedony, once it has been dyed black. In the 1920s and 1930s, it was often used as a substitute for jet.

In this stylized bow dress ring, black onyx has been teamed with diamond.

Above: The raised claw setting holding this brilliant-cut diamond solitaire in place was developed in the 19th century and is used mainly for transparent faceted stones, because it allows a lot of light to enter the exposed stone.

Top: The rectangular-shaped emerald in this ring has rounded terminals.

Above: The central, rectangular-cut diamond in this ring weighs 1.96 carats. It is flanked on either side by navette-cut diamonds. A navette cut is the same as a marquise cut—it is a modification of the brilliant cut being elliptical and pointed at both ends.

ONYX

25

Top: An exquisite example of a brilliant-cut diamond eternity ring.

Above: A very simple, but striking ring made from three brilliant-cut diamonds set on a plain hoop.

Left: This simple ring has a central circular-cut diamond weighing 8.76 carats, with three diamonds on either side, all set on a plain hoop. It was made circa 1925 and valued by Christie's in the US at between $42,000 and $59,000.

Above: This historic ring commemorates the 1823 French intervention of Spain, when a state of anarchy threatened to endanger not only France but also the rest of Europe. Backed by the powers at the Congress of Verona, the Duc d'Angouleme, Louis XVIII's nephew, marched across the border on April 7, and restored order. However, subsequent crises meant that the Spanish monarchy was not restored until the following year.

The portrait on the hinged bezel of the vari-colored gold ring is of the Duc d'Angouleme. The inscription around it is: "L'Europe l'admire L'Espagne le Benit," meaning "Europe admires Spain, the blessed." Meanwhile, the turquoise bead rim opens to reveal a tiny piece of folded paper on which is printed "Composition de l'Armee d'Espagne commandee par S.A.R. le Duc d'Angouleme," which translates as "Piece of writing about the Spanish Army, commissioned by the Duke of Angouleme."

Above: The swiveling bezel of this very early 19th century papal presentation ring carries a sardonyx profile portrait of Pius VII (1742–1823), wearing a rose-cut diamond skull-cap and a chasuble, the border of which is inscribed with the words "Pius VII." The border of the ring is made from rose-cut diamonds. On the reverse, pavé-set in rose-cut diamonds are the Chiaramonti arms (Pius VII was born Gregorio Baranba Chiaramonti), including three small armorial onyx blackamoor (young African) heads and the word "Pax" for "peace." The hoop of the ring is also adorned with rose-cut diamonds.

The most likely recipient of the ring was Prince Nikolai Borisovich Yusupov Senior (1750–1831), who was Catherine the Great's envoy and traveled extensively throughout Europe buying works of art (such as a well-known collection of cameos) for the Russian Empress. Nikolai Yusupov certainly came into contact with the Vatican, because he was responsible for gaining Pius VI's permission to reproduce Raphael's *loggia* (the original being in the Vatican) in the Hermitage, St Petersburg's major art gallery.

27

All seven rings on these pages are good examples of Art Nouveau design.

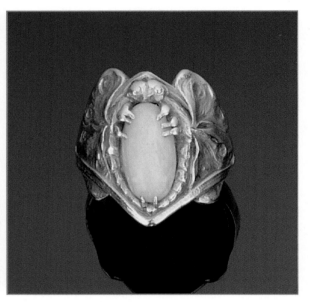

Above: The central oval opal of this ring is held in place by two embracing butterflies, with their wings forming the shoulders. It was made around 1900 by the French firm of Arnould et Cie.

Above Left: A chased flowerhead border surrounds the oval-shaped opal in this turn of the century ring.

Left: This elegant ring features an elongated opal center, with a matted and polished entwined flower bezel with rose-cut diamond detail.

ART NOUVEAU

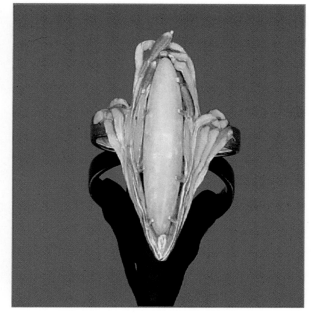

Far Right: This ring, designed by Deluret, has an opal surrounded by a chased flowerhead border. It was made circa 1900.

Right: This unusual looking ring consists of a pear-shaped opal set in a pierced surround with a triple thistle, diamond and enamel surmount. Made circa 1900, it is believed to be of French design and bears the maker's initials M.M.

Above Right: The three translucent green and brown enamel bulrushes in this ring enclose an elongated opal. Created at the beginning of the century, the style of the ring is very much in keeping with that of Albert Vigan.

Above: This beautiful enamel, pearl and diamond ring, made in about 1900, recreates mistletoe in gem form. The *plique a jour* enamel leaves surround a central pearl berry, while the shoulders are set with diamonds.

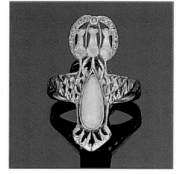

Top Left: In this ring, single baguette-cut diamonds, set on a plain hoop, flank a central cushion-shaped ruby weighing 2.67 carats.

Top Right: This ring features a central circular-cut diamond weighing 2.96 carats, either side of which are three diamonds. The London branch of Christie's valued it at up to £12,000.

Above Left: The 3.94 carat oval-shaped emerald in the center of this ring is supported by single triangular-cut diamond shoulders.

Above Right: The large, 6.17 carat diamond in the center of this ring is flanked on either side by three baguette-cut diamonds. It was thought to be worth up to £28,000.

Above: This knuckle-duster of a ring consists of a central cushion-shaped ruby weighing 8.22 carats surrounded by two rows of brilliant-cut diamonds, with pavé-set diamond shoulders on a plain hoop.

An accompanying certificate from The Gübelin Gemmological Laboratory states that the ruby is of Burmese origin and shows no indication of thermal treatment. This is a major factor in the estimated price of £75,000-95,000.

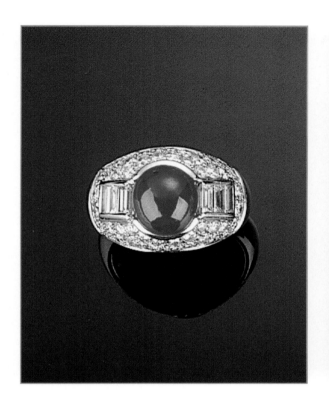

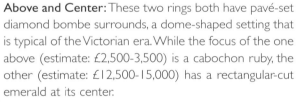

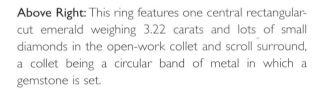

Above and Center: These two rings both have pavé-set diamond bombe surrounds, a dome-shaped setting that is typical of the Victorian era. While the focus of the one above (estimate: £2,500-3,500) is a cabochon ruby, the other (estimate: £12,500-15,000) has a rectangular-cut emerald at its center.

Top Right: This very pretty ring resembles a flower: the central, cushion-shaped ruby represents the stamen, while the brilliant-cut diamonds are the petals.

Above Right: This ring features one central rectangular-cut emerald weighing 3.22 carats and lots of small diamonds in the open-work collet and scroll surround, a collet being a circular band of metal in which a gemstone is set.

Bottom Right: The perfect Valentine's present. A central, heart-shaped diamond weighing 2.06 carats in the midst of a graduated pavé-set diamond heart-shaped surround with pavé-set shoulders. At an estimated price of $7,500-10,500 only the most ardent suitor need attend the auction.

Above: The most interesting feature of this sapphire and diamond cluster ring is the central cushion-shaped sapphire weighing 7.34 carats, because—according to an accompanying certificate from The Swiss Gemmological Institute—it comes from Kashmir and shows no indication of thermal treatment. The size and quality of the gem led Christie's London to estimate the ring's value at up to £22,000.

Kashmiri sapphires were only discovered when a rock slide in a remote corner of the north-western Himalayas revealed sapphire-bearing rock. However, in those early days, sapphires were found in such abundance that the local people thought they were semi-precious stones. It was only when they were examined by the gem merchants of Delhi that their true worth was recognized. The Maharajah of Kashmir immediately took an interest in the sapphires and imposed strict licensing on their mining.

For many years, the exact location of the mines was a closely guarded secret, kept particularly from Europeans, who were always keen to plunder prodigious mining areas. The area was mined up until the 1930s and produced some of the most beautiful sapphires the world has ever seen, but the supply has long since dried up. Now, the only source of Kashmiri sapphires is old jewelry, from which the gems must be removed and, sometimes, re-cut to fit modern settings.

Top: This Art Deco ring could easily be passed off as a cocktail ring—a modern ring that has no fixed form but is large and usually set with a cluster of stones.

The central circular-cut diamond is surrounded by baguette-cut diamond shoulders and a pavé-set diamond border. The French maker's and assay marks—the latter indicating that the gold has been tested to ascertain its purity—date the ring to around 1930.

Above: This solitaire ring, with a diamond weighing 3.24 carats, has ribbed shoulders leading to a plain hoop. Although Christie's did not provide a date for this piece of jewelry, ribbed (also known as reeded or ridged) shoulders were very fashionable up until 1910.

32

Above: The brilliant-cut 3.07 carat diamond in this ring is an "F" on the diamond color scale.

Right: The brilliant-cut diamond in this ring weighs 9.37 carats. Hence the large estimate of £28,000-32,000.

BRILLIANT CUT

Above: This is called a crossover ring because the band of the ring is larger than a full circle, the two terminals overlapping each other. Typically, as in this case, each terminal is studded with a gemstone. One is decorated with a square emerald, while the other supports a cushion-shaped diamond.

Above Right: This rectangular cabochon emerald, surrounded by two rows of diamonds, is set on a plain hoop.

Right: Here we have four sapphire rings of varying styles. The first (top left), with an estimate from the London branch of Christie's of £1,000-1,200, is fairly classic, featuring a sapphire and two diamonds in support. Although the second (top right), has rose-diamond points, it is dominated by five sapphires. The third (bottom left), a cluster ring, is slightly unusual and very modern looking: it involves a central cushion-shaped sapphire surrounded by tapering baton-shaped diamonds that give it an undulating border. The cluster can actually be removed and used as a pendant. The estimate on this ring was £2,500-3,000. The fourth, and final, ring in this group (bottom right) is an oval-shaped sapphire and diamond cluster ring, with an estimate of £500-600, which is not dissimilar in style to the late Princess of Wales's engagement ring.

34

Above: This very angular ring features a cushion-shaped single stone and two-row diamond shoulders.

Above: This diamond cluster ring is not outrageously expensive at an estimated £1,000-1,200, because brownish-yellow diamonds are among the most common of "fancy" diamonds.

Above: The front of this antique ring has an oval blue enamel panel set with three diamonds and a rose-diamond surround, while the back has a locket.

It is not known when the first locket ring was produced, but an example dating to around 1576 has been discovered and is now displayed at the British Prime Minister's country residence, Chequers. While the outside is set with gemstones, two portraits—one of Elizabeth I and the other believed to be of Anne Boleyn—adorn the inside.

Above: The well-known French jewelry house of Cartier mounted this ring, with its two square emeralds and central cushion-shaped diamond.

ANTIQUE

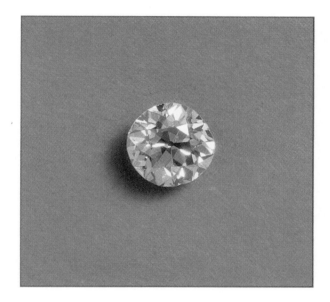

Above: This simple, but stunning, brilliant-cut yellow diamond ring has a carved mount and a plain hoop. The weight of the diamond is 4.50 carats.

Left: Harry Winston created this interesting variation on a cluster ring, which was valued at $280,000-350,000. The, cushion-shaped 21.75 carat sapphire, surrounded by a marquise-cut and pear-shaped diamond cluster, is set on a split platinum hoop. A certificate from the Gübelin Gemmological Laboratory confirms that it is a Kashmiri sapphire and shows no evidence of thermal treatment.

Harry Winston is a very well known American jeweler who was known as the "King of Diamonds" in the 1950s. In 1920, at the age of just 24, Winston opened the Premier Diamond Company in New York City. Twelve years later, he established another company under his own name and was soon cutting such famous diamonds as the "Jonker," the "Taylor-Burton," the "Star of Sierra Leone" and the "Vargas."

Over the years, Winston owned as many as one third of all the famous diamonds in the world, three of which—the "Hope," the "Portuguese" and the "Oppenheimer"—he donated to the Smithsonian. These days, the Harry Winston empire is run by his son, Ronald, who took over as President and CEO of the company on his father's death in 1978. He continues to offer "Rare Jewels of the World," the firm's motto for many years.

JEWELS

Previous pages: Diamond and sapphire bracelet once the property of Vera Hue-Williams. See page 46.

Above: The eight diamond-set charms hanging from this attractive, 19cm long charm bracelet are a heart, car, horseshoe, dog, bird, revolver, fox mask and banjo.

It is thought that charm bracelets first came into existence in the 19th century, but they were not widely worn until the early 20th century. Traditionally, the charms were worn to bring good luck to the wearer and ward off evil spirits, but nowadays, they are more likely to reflect the owner's interests or recent holiday destinations.

A bracelet is a piece of jewelry worn on a wrist or forearm. It is usually made from a flexible band or series of links joined by a clasp, but sometimes it is rigid and, on these occasions, is known as a bangle, rather than a bracelet.

As with rings, both men and women have worn bracelets from very early times, the earliest example known to man dating to the Sumerian civilization around 2500BC. However, in those days, it is thought that they were used not only for adornment but also as a form of money.

While bracelets were very popular among ancient cultures, such as the Egyptians, Greeks and Romans, and right up until the 13th century, their popularity declined in parallel with the power of the Byzantine Empire. The fashion for long sleeves during the Renaissance did nothing to encourage their return.

They enjoyed something of a revival in the 18th and 19th centuries, and by the mid-19th century were the most common form of jewelry. In the 1820s and 1830s, women were wearing several bulky, non-matching bracelets with large jeweled or portrait clusters. As many as five were worn from wrist to elbow. Often the central cluster could be detached and used as a pendant or a brooch.

Toward the end of the 19th century, there was enormous demand for inexpensive bracelets, with large numbers of engraved silver and metal cuff bangles being mass produced. Then came the Art Nouveau era and with it pretty little designs featuring female forms and elements from nature.

The Edwardian era saw a return to more delicate and much thinner bracelets, only one of which was usually worn. However, when sleeveless dresses and the shedding of evening gloves became popular in the 1920s, the wearing of several bracelets at the same time was *de rigueur*. Cartier and Van Cleef & Arpels both produced particularly good examples of bracelets at this time.

The 1920s also witnessed the start of modern jewelry—with bracelets produced out of material other than precious metals. For example, glass and Bakelite plastic came to prominence.

Since the Second World War, no particular feature has restricted bracelet design. There are avant-garde designers producing unique pieces and there are manufacturers mass producing bracelets using silver and semi-precious stones, rather than gold and gems, so it is always possible for buyers to find something to suit their style and price range.

These days, in the West at least, bracelets are mostly worn by women, while in the East many men still wear them too. They can be worn on the left or right wrist, or both, with no symbolism being attached to their positioning. In addition, either one or several may be worn, there is no set etiquette.

Left: When the price of a piece of jewelry isn't even listed in the Christie's catalog, a very expensive price tag is guaranteed. This Art Deco emerald, sapphire, diamond and onyx bracelet is such a piece. The Aga Khan III, the hereditary head of the Ismailian sect of Muslims, asked the French jewelry house of Cartier to create this bracelet in 1930.

The central focus of the bracelet is the rectangular-cut 76 carat emerald, which is engraved with a surah from the *Qur'an*. The pierced bracelet band is made of engraved emerald and sapphire leaves and brilliant-cut diamond springs, which have been enhanced by small cuts of black onyx. The Art Deco blend of blue and green was a Cartier specialty.

The Aga Khan III became a patron of Cartier, Paris in 1902. From the very beginning his purchases were noted for their avant-garde use of color, which pointed to the revolutionary designs of the future Art Deco movement.

Left: This pair of antique ruby, emerald and rose-cut diamond bracelets, with their expanding trellis design, was made around 1880.

A rose-cut is a symmetrical form, with facets of various shapes and relative sizes, that characteristically has a flat base and two horizontal rows of facets rising to a point. The style, which was developed by Dutch lapidaries in the mid-17th century, lost popularity in the 18th, but once again found favor at the end of the last century.

Left: This 17.9cm long diamond bracelet, with its stylised buckle design and central lozenge-shaped panel (with flexible open circle terminals on a scroll-link band) is typical of the pieces created in the Art Deco ago. It is signed by Cartier.

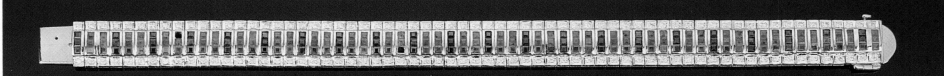

Above: This 17.8cm long bracelet of alternate calibré-cut sapphires, rubies and emeralds, with a brilliant-cut diamond line border includes every precious stone known to man.

Above Left: This unusual 17.8cm long silver bracelet has rectangular hinged links, the middle sections of which are set with square cabochon amethysts. The bracelet was designed by the jewelry house of Carlo Giuliano some time between 1863 and 1896, because it bears the mark "CG"—all pieces designed after that time bear the initials "C & AG," after Carlo and Arthur Giuliano, the two sons who took over the business in 1896.

Carlo Giuliano senior, who started the jewelry house, hailed from Naples, but made his mark in London, where his encrusted enameling and work in granulated gold were highly regarded. He was renowned for the jewelry he created that was based on his own interpretation of ancient Etruscan styles, but he also designed pieces in neo-Renaissance, Egyptian Revival and Indian styles.

Center Left: The Parisian jeweler Jules Wièse is known for his architecturally styled pieces and this 17cm long bracelet is no exception, reflecting Gothic style.

The hexagonal-shaped centerpiece of the bracelet is a diamond cluster on a pierced gold panel above deep blue enamel, which is pinned with pearls at the rims. The four oblong flanking links are decorated in a similar style with pearl-set baluster intersections and there is a pearl-set safety-chain.

The mark of two stars on the clasp was valid from 1844 to 1890, but the bracelet is believed to have been made circa 1866. Other marks include the initials J.W. (for Jules Wièse) and an oblong double punch similar to the one registered by Froment-Meurice in 1866. This would make sense, as Jules Wièse is known to have studied under and worked for F.D. Froment-Meurice and his son. Their joint names appear, therefore, on a number of jewels, but it is not known to what extent Froment-Meurice's workshop manufactured jewelry and to what extent they used outside suppliers

Another interesting mark on the bracelet is the double mark used for plated items that does not appear in the register of hallmarks in the Bureau de la Garantie

in Paris. French or "double" gold was inspired by Sheffield plate, but the gold coating covered the copper core rather than being fused to it and rolled to the copper ingot as in the Sheffield process. This technique was so successful that Birmingham goldsmiths, who called it "rolled gold," adopted it.

Below Left: This beautiful 17.5cm long bracelet, which Christie's, London gave an estimated price of £50,000-70,000, is made from five South Sea cultured pearls (measuring between 15.54mm and 18.58mm in diameter), all set within brilliant-cut diamond surrounds, which have marquise and brilliant-cut diamond spacers.

Below: This graduated flexible bracelet, set with three-rows of cushion-cut diamonds, was made around 1935 and measures 17.5cm long.

Bottom: This 18cm long flexible bracelet is set with cabochon sapphires (of varying shades of blue) and small diamond collet details. Despite the fact that three sapphires are missing, Christie's still placed on estimate of £8,000 to £12,000 on the bracelet.

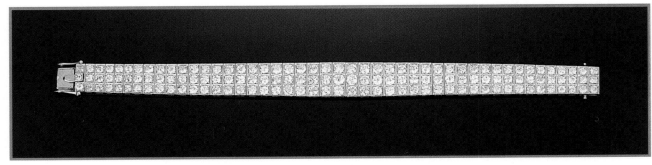

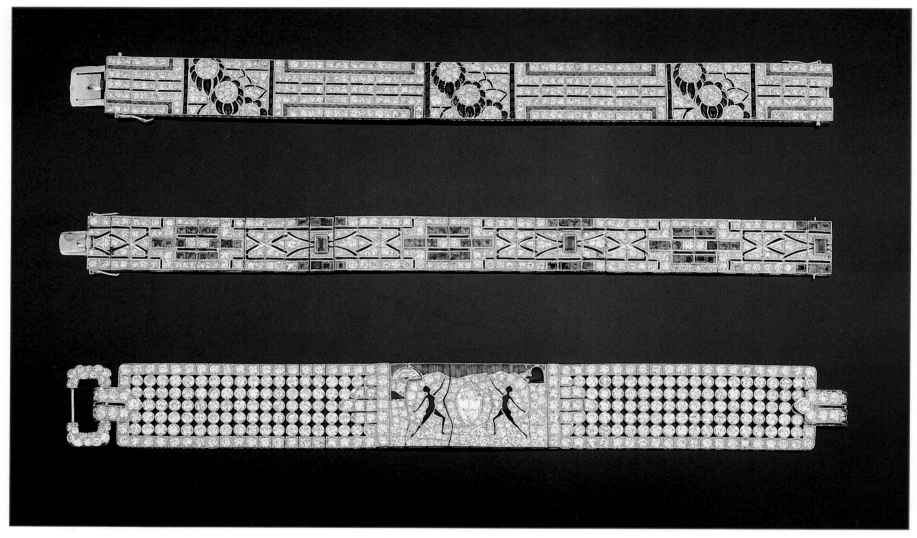

The above three bracelets are fine examples of Art Deco jewelry that were sold by Christie's on behalf of an avid collector.

Top: This 17.8cm long bracelet has three pierced onyx and diamond foliate rectangular panels flanked by calibré-cut onyx borders with pierced diamond and calibré-cut ruby lines. French assay and maker's marks date the piece to circa 1925.

Center: Slightly longer at 18.2cm is this emerald and diamond bracelet of pierced geometric design. It, too, was created in about 1925.

Above: The third bracelet is quite rare, a fact reflected in its estimated price of £25,000-28,000.

Within the central rectangular pavé-set diamond pierced panel, two black enamel dancers can be seen flanking the central marquise-cut diamond. In the background, there is a calibré-cut sapphire sky and lunette-cut diamond sun, as well as a black onyx heart.

A diamond vertical line border separates the panel from graduated palmette shoulders and five rows of flexible collets set within a single-line diamond border. The bracelet is held in place with a buckle panel clasp.

Left: This very simple Tiffany bracelet features a single line of gems that alternates between five rectangular-cut sapphires and five circular-cut diamonds. Made in about 1920, it is 18cm long and is signed "Tiffany & Co."

The American jewelry house of Tiffany was founded in 1837 by Charles Louis Tiffany, who originally acted only as a retailer, selling the jewelry that he had sourced from Europe. However, in 1848, the company started manufacturing its own jewelry and rose to prominence in the 20th century when a number of great designers were employed to produce their own signature lines.

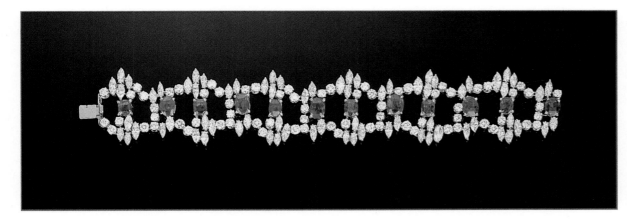

Left: This rather pretty Frohmann bracelet was made circa 1965 from a series of 12 cushion-shaped pink sapphires, edged by an undulating border of brilliant and navette-cut diamonds and diamond collet intersections. Estimate: £15,000-20,000

Left: Diamond bracelets do not come much simpler than this. Set with 55 princess-cut diamonds, it measures 18cm long.

These days, a princess cut is known as a profile cut. Essentially, it involves making the most out of small piece of gemstone by cutting it so that it has a large surface area and good internal reflection, but very little depth.

TIFFANY

Above: The most interesting aspect of this bracelet is its provenance: it was once the property of the socialite Vera Hue-Williams.

Born Vera Sklarevskia in Kiev at the turn of the century, she fled the Russian Revolution, along with her sister Olga and her mother Baroness Kostovesky, in 1917, arriving in Paris with very few possessions other than the jewels hidden in her clothes.

At 17, the stunningly beautiful Vera married an Englishman, who died ten years later. Her second husband, Walter Sherwin Cottingham, whom she married in 1931, owned the Lewis Berger Paint Company. When he died five years later, she inherited his fortune. During the Second World War, Vera married Thomas Lilley, chairman of the shoe company Lilley & Skinner. Together, they set up the Woolton House Stud at their home in Woolton Hill near Newbury. Even in the glamorous world of horse racing, Vera was a leading light. Not only that, she was also a winner. Her horses triumphed in several important races, including the first running of the King George VI and Queen Elizabeth Stakes in 1951. Four years after Lilley died in 1959, Vera

wed—for the fourth and final time—Colonel Roger Hue-Williams, who was to die in 1987.

Throughout her life, Vera traveled extensively, visiting friends, attending to her business interests and holidaying in some of the world's most exclusive resorts. All these activities demanded glamorous clothes and expensive jewels. And Vera's jewelry, much of it designed and made in the 1930s, was always of the finest quality even if the design was very simple.

The impressive bracelet, made in the 1930s from a flexible pavé-set and baguette-cut diamond tapered band down the center of which run 18 slightly graduated rectangular-cut sapphires, measures 17.8cm long. The total weights of the sapphires and diamonds are approximately 64 and 27 carats respectively. Christie's estimated its value, before it was auctioned, at $150,000 to $170,000.

Above Right: This Cartier bracelet has six cabochon emeralds mounted within a diamond open running scroll band. Its price, estimated by Christie's in London, is a relatively modest £10,000 to £12,000.

Bangles, such as these, differ from bracelets in that they are rigid.

Above: These two Cartier bangles, which were expected to reach up to $100,000 at auction depict the chimera, a fire breathing monster that appeared in various forms in the ancient art of the Mediterranean (most importantly in Greek mythology), India, China and Africa.

It was Jacques Cartier who first had the idea of producing chimera jewelry. Traveling through India, he became aware of the Indian variant whose origin pre-dates that of Greek iconography. The *makara* is based on the Indian crocodile, which first appeared in Indian art in the 3rd century. However, from the 17th century onward, the snout of the *makara* became gradually more and more elongated until the crocodile resembled an elephant, and it is this shape that Cartier reproduced. It is also possible that Cartier was influenced by the work of the 19th century jewelers Fortunato Pio Castellani and Eugene Fontenay, both of whom used Greek mythology as an influence in their work.

The bangles took up to 300 hours to produce and are so beautifully sculpted that they could almost be an *objet d'art*. The coral, specially imported from Japan, had to be thick enough to enable the craftsmen to carve a whole bangle out in one piece.

The fact that these bangles are larger than most sets them apart, as does the square cross-section. One has rotating chimera head terminals with cabochon emerald and pavé-set diamond details. The other, which is very similar in design, only has a single rotating terminal.

The chimera was certainly one of Cartier's most successful creations, appearing not only as bracelets but also on clocks, boxes and various artifacts. However, the bangles were the most popular item, retaining their popularity right up until the 1960s—this pair was made around 1965.

Above Right: These four diamond bangles look as though they could be one, so snugly do they fit together. Each one is set with brilliant-cut diamonds and is 6.5cm wide. All are signed by the French jewelry house of Fred, hence why they also have French assay marks.

Below Right: This Victorian gold bangle, which resembles a wristwatch, has a detachable locket (inside which is a glazed compartment) that has been enameled in dark blue. The tapering strap is engraved with flowers and foliage. Dating to around 1830, the bangle is 17.7cm long.

47

NECKLACES

Above: This attractive diamond choker, with its black velvet band and garlanded leaves and flowers, is typically Edwardian.

Previous pages: An Indian gem-set and enamel fringe necklace.

A necklace is a flexible piece of jewelry worn around the neck. They have been worn throughout the ages. Necklaces tend to be loose, rather than close-fitting like a choker or long like a sautoir and the term encompasses many different styles, such as festoon, fringe, bib and bead necklaces, many of which are described in this chapter.

The first known example of a necklace was found in the grave of the Sumerian Queen Pu-abi who died around 2500BC—it was gold and simple in design. During the Egyptian era, broad collar necklaces were popular and in Roman times, beaded necklaces were all the rage.

As early as the Byzantine age, necklaces were being produced from gold and precious stones. In the Middle Ages, it was popular for reliquaries, cameos and intaglios to be hung from chains. Pendants then became popular again at the end of the 18th and beginning of the 19th century, when empire line dresses provided the perfect platform for a pendant necklace.

They tend to divide quite nicely into two categories: those worn simply for decoration and those worn for a purpose, be it religious or magical, in which case the wearer may not even display the pendant, but keep it hidden under clothing.

Pendants worn as ornaments can be any shape or size, but are often made from either gold or silver decorated with enamel, gems or a combination of the two. Pendants with a purpose might be

an amulet to ward off evil spirits, a locket containing a picture of a loved one or a cross denoting religious devotion.

From the 16th century onward, the necklace took on many different forms as fashions fluctuated. For example, in the mid-16th century, high necklines were popular with the result that necklaces were made longer. One hundred years later, the necklines and necklaces were reversed.

During the Baroque age, the bow was a recurrent theme in jewelry. In the 1760s, necklaces, which tended to be a simple row of pearls or a jeweled garland of ribbons and flowers, were worn high on the neck, sometimes with a lower neckchain known as an *esclavage*. In the 1770s and 1780s, festoon necklaces, which covered the bosom and filled the low necklines of court dresses, were very fashionable.

At the start of the 19th century, the neoclassical style was popular. Necklaces were made from a single string of precious stones or pearls, from which hung a series of pendants—the first fringe necklace.

Closely fitting necklaces are referred to either as chokers or dog collars. If there is any difference between the two terms, it is that chokers tend to be narrower than dog collars and sometimes have a pendant attached.

Chokers, although they had been in use since the 16th century, first enjoyed real recognition in

the Victorian age when they were made from ribbon decorated with gems. Later, multiple rows of pearls became popular, some of them with an elaborate central ornament known as a *plaque de cou* (neck badge). Chokers then hit a peak in the 1900s, when Queen Alexandra, the Danish consort of King Edward VII, took to wearing them with long bead necklaces because—it was said—she had a scar on her neck.

Although sautoirs first made their mark in the 19th century, they became really popular in the early 1920s. Worn loosely from the shoulders, a sautoir usually extended somewhere below the waist and might have either a jeweled pendant or tassel at its lowest point. Sometimes, a sautoir would be worn over only one shoulder, in a military style.

Their popularity in the 1920s stemmed from changing fashions: dresses, instead of having a corseted hourglass silhouette, were knee-length and loose fitting, and highly coiffed hair gave way to the crop. By elongating their necklaces, women hoped to create a more becoming line from neck to waist, which emphasized the femininity that they felt had somehow been sacrificed to their boyish, short hair.

Jewelry for the neck produced since the Second World War has taken on many forms, but the most popular have been collars, pendant necklaces and rigid metal chokers, some with pendants attached.

CHOKERS

Above: The focus of this very pretty choker is the diamond collet and open leaf work center, which can be detached and used as a brooch (the necessary extra fitting is supplied). The center is held in place by a 16-row pearl necklace, which has two diamond bar dividers and a diamond bar clasp.

Below: The diamond framed panel at the front of this Art Nouveau choker necklace features open-work *plique a jour*. This enameling technique involves outlining the design in metal and then filling it in with enamel—as there is no backing, the enamel takes on an appearance similar to that of a stained glass window. This method was used in the Renaissance era and enjoyed something of a comeback at the turn of the century.

The panel is held in place by a choker made from 16 rows of seed pearls (small round pearls weighing less than one quarter of a grain, a grain being the unit of weight for pearls and equaling one quarter of a gemstone carat).

OPEN LEAF

51

Top: This antique choker, dating to 1860, is made from 22 open-work diamond foliate and scroll elongated panels separated by cushion-cut diamond collet spacers. Mounted in silver and gold, it is 37cm long when worn as a necklace, but divides into two to form two bracelets. It comes in a fitted case with the name S.J. Rood & Co. embossed on it and was estimated to be worth up to $33,000.

Above: This *Belle Époque* choker consists of a pearl latticework collar with diamond foliate spacers, at the center of which is a pear-shaped pierced diamond panel set with circular-cut diamonds that suspends a pearl drop.

Right: Another *Belle Époque* choker, this one created in 1905 by Cartier and sold by Christie's (where it was valued at $42,000 to $67,000) with a certificate of authenticity from the jewelry house and its original green leather fitted case.

This is an excellent example of Louis Cartier's visionary jewelry. Very much in the garland style, the choker has lines of diamond collets interspersed with rose-cut diamond laurel leaves, among which are studded old European-cut diamond pendant details. His adoption of a platinum mount was revolutionary, being preferable to the cumbersome, highly malleable and easily tarnished silver mounts of the 18th century.

Instead of following the dictates of the Art Nouveau movement that was dominant at the time, Cartier adopted the delicate garland style, which was largely inspired by 18th century French Louis XVI motifs. The result was a light and highly flexible platinum mount of great beauty and sophistication.

The exquisite choker was presented to Principessa Giulia Branciforte Lanza di Trabia e di Butera (1870–1947) by her husband, head of one of the grand families of Sicily, Pietro Branciforte, Principe Lanza di Trabia e di Butera (1862–1920), on the occasion of their 20th wedding anniversary. They had married on December 6, 1885, in Palermo, when she was only 15. The couple traveled frequently and it was probably during one of their many trips to Paris that the Prince visited the Cartier showroom on Rue de la Paix and selected the choker. His choice certainly reflects the best of what contemporary and fashionable *haute joaillerie* was offering at that time.

Principessa Giulia's two daughters, Principessa Sofia Borghese (1896–1984), Dama di Palazzo of H.M. the Queen Elena of Italy, and Principessa Giovanna Moncada di Paterno (1897–1985), inherited the choker and it remained in the family until it was sold through Christie's. Very rarely does such a beautiful *Belle Époque* jewel, in its original state and in very good condition, make an appearance at auction.

52

CARTIER

NECKLACES

Right: This jade festoon necklace is made from graduated carved jade oval plaque collets with trefoil leaf intersections, from which seven similar drops hang.

The term "jade" is used to describe the two minerals jadeite and nephrite. Jadeite is the superior of the two, but its quality does vary. The rarest and most valuable type is a translucent deep emerald or grassy green, which is known as "emerald jade" because of its close resemblance to the precious stone. However, it is far rarer and much more expensive than emerald.

Below Right: This could be considered a forerunner to today's costume jewelry, if it were not for the fact that it is a rare and early enameled gold and gem-set necklace.

Enamel (a pigment usually composed of powdered potash and silica, bound with oil and colored with metallic oxides) has been in use in Egypt since 1600BC and extensively in Europe from the 16th century.

This piece dates to about 1620. Its pierced gold oblong links, alternately enameled in black and white, are set with red stones of no particular origin. The links, once used as dress ornaments, are older than the quatrefoil rings that link them. The necklace can be split into two bracelets.

Far Right: This 43.2cm long necklace, a rare and important piece made circa 1620, also features enamel, alongside gold and diamonds.

All the open-work links are enameled in blue, black and green, with raised dotted enamel decorating the crown-shaped crests and diamond drops. The center of each link has a small table-cut diamond in a square collet setting, on the reverse of which there is colored peapod enameling.

Lady Margaret Napier (born circa 1620) wore a similar necklace when George Jamesone painted her. That portrait is now in the Stirling of Keir Collection in the Scottish National Portrait Gallery Archives.

ENAMEL

53

Above: This rather interesting Art Deco necklace was made around 1925 by the firm of Lacloche Frères. The front section consists of six rows of graduated ruby beads separated by diamond star spacers, which hang from rectangular-cut ruby and diamond open-work scroll terminals. The back features two rows of ruby beads with diamond star spacers and a cabochon ruby and diamond scroll clasp.

Originally Spanish, Lacloche Frères was founded in Madrid in 1875 by four brothers, Fernand, Jules, Leopold and Jacques. They subsequently opened branches in San Sebastian, Biarritz, Paris and London. Highly successful during the 1920s and 1930s, their specialty was jewelry and *objets d'art* decorated with enamels and carved gemstones. This piece was valued in London at about £20,000-30,000.

Right: This necklace is of particular interest because it is another piece that was once the property of the socialite Vera Hue-Williams. It is unusual because it is more fussy than most of Vera's jewels.

A pear-shaped, marquise and baguette-cut diamond cluster surrounds the central cushion-shaped ruby pendant. Meanwhile the graduated cushion-shaped ruby necklace is littered with cushion-shaped ruby, baguette and French-cut diamond bow intersections and ends in a baguette-cut diamond bow clasp.

Made in around 1935, this 40cm long necklace comes with a certificate from the Gübelin Gemmological Laboratory stating that the main ruby (weighing 14.81 carats) is of Burmese origin and shows no evidence of thermal treatment. The total weights of the other rubies and diamonds are approximately 195 and 39 carats, respectively. Christie's estimate was a colossal $830,000 to $1,200,000.

54

ART DECO

Above: This Cartier necklace, which Christie's, London expected to fetch between £50,000-60,000 was made at the turn of the century, but you probably would not think it if you were judging its age by its style, which is very much 18th century.

Many interior and decorative designers remained faithful to the Louis XVI style long after it had passed into history, because the upper echelons of society in England, France and America still liked the elegance and ceremony associated with the 18th century court. Cartier was one of the jewelry houses that created pieces in this style from 1895 onward, and it did so with greater skill than the competition. The main reason for this was Cartier's use of the best platinum in Paris, which gave its designers new technical freedom and allowed the 18th century inspired pieces to take on a spirit not previously seen in the jeweler's art.

This necklace consists of a series of seven oval-shaped sapphire and diamond clusters, each supporting a foliate festoon with a pear-shaped sapphire and diamond cluster drop. In between the clusters are graduated diamond collet intersections.

Above Right: This rather fun, 44cm long necklace is made from a series of pavé-set diamond elephants with cabochon ruby eyes.

LOUIS XVI

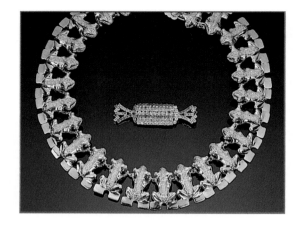

Below Right: This delicate necklace is made from a series of triangular and pear-shaped amethysts connected by pearl-set scroll lattice links.

Center From Top to Bottom

This 40cm long necklace features pre-Columbian stylized frogs (as if ready to leap) anddecorative scrolls.

Pre-Columbian style relates to jewelry made by the American Indians before the arrival of Columbus in 1492 and thereafter until the conquest in the 16th century by the Spanish Conquistadors, hence why the style is sometimes also called pre-Hispanic. The style tended to reflect indigenous forms, such as these frogs.

This Carlo Giuliano necklace is not as it would have been when it was made in around 1880—the central pendant is missing. What remains are two six-stranded sections (only one of which is visible in the picture), measuring 17.6cm long in total, which have partly pierced gold and black and white enamel panels at either end with hook fasteners. Two of these panels have diamonds (the pierced areas lacking some enamel).

This necklace is made from ten pear-shaped amber beads, in between which lie rondelle spacers. A rondelle is a thin, circular piece of metal or gemstone that has been pierced so that it can be strung on a necklace. In this case, the rondelles are flat slices of faceted diamond.

This historic festoon necklace is dotted with enamel portraits of Louis XVI and Marie Antoinette, plus other important figures from the French court, such as the Duchesse d'Angouleme and Madame Elizabeth. On the flipsides of the portraits are *grisaille* studies—*grisaille* being a kind of enameling in monochrome. The portraits are mounted between chains made either from seed pearls, enameled *fleurs-de-lis* or flowers.

Although this type of jewelry was very popular in the 18th century, this necklace was actually made circa 1890, when Empress Eugenie, wife of Napoleon III, once again made the style popular.

Christie's sold the necklace in its original red leather fitted case.

Far Right: This Italian gold and Roman micro-mosaic, 44cm long fringe necklace was created in the late 19th century, with the quality of the mosaics indicating that it was probably around 1860.

Twelve of the mosaics depict the caesars, while the thirteenth (right in the center, at the front of the necklace, with the inscription "SPQR" above it) is the personification of Rome. The soft coloring of the Caesars, who have their name inscribed above their profile, is reminiscent of Roman frescoes.

The portraits are set in wirework mounts, which have beaded projections and pendant floral mosaics in shield shapes, and are strung together by links that have black and white Cupid mosaics which imitate cameos. The circular wirework clasp has a beaded rosette.

All in all, this really is a tour de force of revivalist jewellery. The price indicated by Christie's in London was £18,000-22,000.

FESTOON

Above: The largest sapphire in this very glamorous fringe necklace weighs 31.80 carats. It hangs from a front section of two rows of cushion-shaped sapphires, two of which weigh 10.21 and 11.02 carats. In between the sapphires are diamond collet trefoil and cluster details, and marquise-cut diamond spacers. The single row back chain is held together by a sapphire and diamond cluster clasp.

In accompanying certificates from The Swiss Gemmological Institute, it states that the sapphires weighing 10.21 and 31.80 carats come from Sri Lanka and this is one reason that the London branch of Christie's estimated the piece at £340,000-500,000.

Left: The highlight of this exotic Cartier necklace is the fringe of carved coral flowers, with pearl, old European and single-cut diamond, black onyx, coral and emerald bead cluster centers, that are attached to the coral and black onyx bead necklace by black enamel caps and diamond bars. Mounted in platinum, the necklace was made circa 1940 and was valued at $50,000-58,000.

Top, Center: From the deep blue, red, green and white enameled links of this 37cm long necklace hang oval citrine collets.

Made around 1900, the necklace's double scroll clasp bears the initials C.& A.G. for Carlo and Arthur Giuliano, the two sons who took over the business of their father Carlo in 1896. It was Carlo senior who made the company famous for expert enameling.

Above, Center: This is a black cultured pearl and diamond necklace, with two pavé-set diamond crossover panel connections and a diamond-set clasp, designed by Verdura.

Verdura is a jewelry house set up by the Italian Fulco Santostefano della Cerda, Duke of Verdura, in 1939. Prior to that, he had worked in Paris, first as a textile and then as a jewelry designer for the legendary Coco Chanel. Moving to the United States in 1937, he became a designer for the jeweler Paul Flato, before opening his own salon two years later.

Verdura's jewelry featured gold mountings with precious and semi-precious stones, a bold undertaking at a time when platinum reigned supreme. In 1972, Verdura sold his business and retired to London, where he lived until his death in 1978. The company still exists today, producing fine jewels from Verdura's original drawings.

Top, Right: This 35cm long, flexible graduated bib necklace is set with cabochon sapphires of varying shades of blue.

Above, Right: Cesare Barro created this unusual necklace, featuring a brown topaz briolette-cut drop suspended from a series of topaz circular links with ruby details.

Barro is a contemporary Venetian artist living and working in Rome. Before turning his creative talents to jewelry, he lived for 13 years on the small Greek island of Tinos, where he was a painter and sculptor. His ornate jewels tend to be sold by private appointment in Rome or through exhibitions held throughout Europe, Asia and America.

A briolette cut—as can be seen in this photograph—has no table (large flat facet) and is drop-shaped with a pointed apex and rounded bottom. Topaz is an aluminium silicate that is fairly rare and, therefore, good examples can be costly. Used since the late 18th century because of its brilliant color and lustrous clarity, it comes in various different shades including pink and blue. However, the most sought after color is light sherry brown, not unlike the color of the topaz in this necklace.

Right: This is an adaptable piece of late 19th century jewelry. While it can be worn (as it is seen in the photograph) as a six-row pearl necklace, the octagonal-cut sapphire and cushion-cut diamond cluster clasp is detachable, so that it can also be worn as a brooch. Mounted in silver and gold, the necklace is 38cm long.

Far Right: This 46.5cm long necklace is made of three rows of South Sea cultured pearls, measuring from approximately 9.5mm to 13.2mm in diameter.

Right: This very pretty Victorian necklace is composed of a series of five graduated cushion-shaped ruby and diamond clusters, with ruby and diamond collet foliate and scroll surmounts, which are interspersed with graduated diamond collets suspended from a line of ruby and diamond clusters. The back chain is made from graduated diamond collets, and has a ruby and diamond cluster clasp. The most expensive of the pieces on this page it was valued at £40,000-60,000.

Above, Inner: The focal point of this simple necklace is the five marquise-cut diamond clusters resembling flowers, which are attached to the single line of graduated baguette-cut diamonds by brilliant-cut diamond quatrefoil connections.

Above, Outer: This 38cm long, graduated flexible panel necklace, set with brilliant-cut diamonds, is signed by De Laneau.

Above Right: You would not expect Audrey Hepburn, the elegant star of the silver screen, to have worn anything less stylish than this single row of cultured pearls with a cushion-shaped sapphire and diamond cluster clasp. The cultured pearls measure from around 8.6mm to 9mm in diameter.

Hepburn was born Eda van Heemstra in Brussels in 1929. Although she trained as a ballerina, she went on to win widespread acclaim for her acting and will always be remembered as one of the greatest Hollywood stars. She first enchanted international audiences when she played the runaway Princess Anne in *Roman Holiday* (1953). This was followed by outstanding performances as Eliza Doolittle in *My Fair Lady* (1964) and Holly Golightly in *Breakfast at Tiffany's* (1961). She was nominated for an Oscar five times, winning twice, and was awarded the French award of "Chevalier des Arts et des Lettres." In later years, she became a Goodwill Ambassador for UNICEF, the United Nations' Children's Fund. She died in 1993.

Right: This Cartier necklace was designed as a series of seven oval cabochon emerald, diamond and baguette-diamond open loop clusters with a central tear-shaped drop, all set on a diamond and baguette-diamond single-line back chain. Its estimated value was £15,000-18,000.

61

Right: The blue diamond in this necklace, known as the "Begum Blue," is a magnificent heart-shaped deep blue and weighs 13.78 carats. It, along with the heart-shaped white diamond weighing 16.03 carats, can be detached from the main necklace, which is a graduated heart-shaped diamond line. Designed by Poiray, the necklace is 35cm long.

Accompanying certificates from the Gemmological Institute of America state that the Begum Blue is a natural fancy deep blue and has Vs2 clarity, while the largest white diamond is "D" color and has internal flawless clarity. As you would expect, this is a very expensive piece of jewelry—Christie's did not place an estimate on it meaning that bidding was expected to be fierce and the price astronomical.

Right: This platinum-mounted necklace, estimated at $100,000-130,000 and signed by Van Cleef & Arpels, has two overlapping V-shaped ribbons, each one with graduated baguette, circular, marquise-cut and pear-shaped diamonds. The total estimated weight of the diamonds is 90 carats.

Van Cleef & Arpels, founded in 1906, revolutionized jewelry design by introducing the "invisible setting," when gemstones are mounted without any visible sign of a setting, in 1935. In response to a more casual lifestyle, the company also introduced a "Boutique" range in 1954, a concept which has subsequently been copied by other jewelers.

PLATINUM-MOUNTED

SAUTOIRS

Right: This lattice work sautoir, with pearls, diamond collets and diamond panel shoulders (which can be converted into clips), has a flexible flared pendant hanging from a diamond open circle and two panel mounts.

Right: This charming sautoir has two rows of graduated pearls (ranging in diameter from 5mm to 11.5mm), some large cultured pearls that were added at a later date and a pierced diamond half-moon clasp. With a length of 116cms, it is by far the longest of the sautoirs featured in this book. Its estimate was £20,000-30,000.

Right: The four rows of ruby beads in this sautoir are studded with diamond openwork panels that have a central pavé-set ruby and diamond heart-shaped center. Christie's in London valued it at between £13,000 and £15,000.

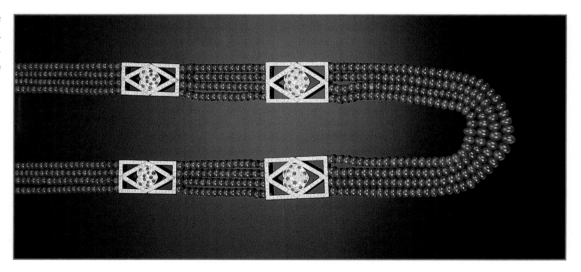

PENDANTS & PENDANT NECKLACES

Cruciform pendants like the ones on these pages, were usually made in a Latin cross or a cross with four arms of equal length and were decorated with engravings or set with gemstones.

Right: This slightly larger pendant cross is set with nine foiled rectangular and oval-shaped emeralds on a chased bi-colored ground with diamond detail. The reverse is engraved.

Below Right: This 5.8cm long cross, made in around 1860, is enameled with a Holbeinesque pattern in red, blue, green and white and features a central pearl flanked by square collet diamond arms. The *en suite*, pearl-set chain has six pierced and enameled links.
The distinctive enameling on the cross is similar to the work done by C.F. Hancock, the London jewelry house responsible for creating the "Devonshire Parure."

Below Center: This 6.5cm long pendant cross, created circa 1840, features a series of six rectangular-cut emeralds with diamond collet terminals and a diamond-set loop. It is presented in a contemporary red leather bound case.

Below Far Right: The engraving, "From V.A. to V.M. 1876," on the reverse of this gold and amethyst cruciform pendant gives an indication of its interesting provenance. Princess Victoria, later the Empress Frederick of Prussia and Queen Victoria's eldest daughter, gave it to her niece, Victoria Melita, second daughter of Alfred, Duke of Edinburgh, Queen Victoria's second son, and his wife Maria, daughter of Alexander II of Russia.

A stunning piece of jewelry, it was created by Ernesto Rinzi in the year that Princess Victoria presented it to her niece. Rinzi is thought to have been brought to London by Alessandro Castellani, a world-famous jeweler in the 19th century. Certainly his work is close to that of Carlo Giuliano, who is known to have worked for Castellani.

Left: This 7.5cm high circular pendant, with a Jean Petitot (1609–91) miniature of Louis XIV (1643–1715) surrounded by large rose-cut diamonds and smaller stones at the outer edges, is very rare. Not many were made because—according to existing evidence—the pendants were used as diplomatic presents.

A similar piece was presented to the Netherlands diplomat Anthonie Heinsuis (1641–1720) by Louis XIV and is now in the Hague Museum. It came from the Registre du Presents du Roi (the Register of the King's presents) and was made by the king's jeweler, M. Montarsy. Two others are known to exist: one belongs to the church of Santa Maria della Vita in Bologna and the other (with a Petitot miniature of William III) is in the Royal Collection. Contemporary documents refer to the pendants as *boites a portraits*, probably because they originally came in outer cases, and a sketch book in the Museum Boymans-Van Beuningen, Rotterdam inextricably links the original design with Thomas Cletscher (1598–1668).

The reverse of this particular pendant, which was made in around 1680, is enameled "in the manner of Thomas Cletscher" and features Louis XIV's cypher on light blue ground, bordered by pink and black flowers and scrolls on a white ground.

Above Left: This very delicate Edwardian diamond pendant features a central circular cluster with a garland surround and pierced diamond detail, all of which is framed by a millegrain (metal beading) border. The pendant hangs on a diamond-set spectacle-link chain.

Above Center: This silver cruciform pendant of open-work form, set with rubies and small diamonds in raised settings, has a matching button and brooch-pin.

Above: This diamond flowerspray pendant, estimated at $51,000-67,000, is mounted *en pampilles*, a term that refers to the cascade of gemstones hanging from the main body of the pendant. The central, cushion-cut diamond in the flowerspray weighs 4.36 carats and has a diamond foliate surround. Above it are a diamond bow and three flowers, the one in the center set with a cushion-cut diamond weighing 5.17 carats. The pendant is mounted in silver and gold, and was made around 1850.

This piece has a long and interesting provenance. It was originally part of the dowry of Louise, Princess of the Netherlands, when she married Carl XV of Sweden and Norway in 1850. It was then given to their daughter, Princess Loise, who married King Frederik VIII of Denmark, and their son Prince Harald, who married Princess Helene of Slesvig-Holsten Sonderborg. Ingeborg Holm, who was married to Consul Christian Holm, subsequently bought the pendant from Princess Helene. They gave it to their daughter Astrid, who married K.F.S. Count Ahlefeldt-Laurvig Eriksholm. She gave it to their grandchild William Ahlefeldt-Laurvig Eriksholm.

Right, from Top to Bottom

This rather elegant Edwardian diamond, sapphire and emerald flexible pendant, which measures 5.7cm high, is made of a tapering acanthus leaf and collet design—a collet being a circular band of metal in which a gemstone is set.

The focus of this circular pendant are the four cabochon moonstones, in between which tiny rubies have been set. The other main features of this pendant are a minutely enameled black and white open-work border, a suspension loop and a pearl drop.
Moonstone, a white translucent form of feldspar, is almost always cut *en cabochon*, which results in a sheen that is bluish on the finest stones and whitish on the more common stones with thicker layers.
Made by Carlo & Arthur Giuliano (1895–1912), the pendant is signed and presented in its original case, which bears the address of 115 Piccadilly. Giuliano's original cases are exquisitely crafted objects in their own right, and a piece in its original case is especially desirable.

This delicate, but intricate, necklace—with a pendant *en suite*—has pearl-set links between translucent green foliage dotted with small diamonds and set against white enamel scrolls. The actual pendant has ribbon bow cresting and a demantoid garnet, the most valuable type of garnet having many similarities to diamond (hence its name demantoid, meaning diamond-like) which was discovered in the 1860s.
The necklace was made in the late 19th century and comes in a fitted case bearing the retailer's address of London & Ryder, which was at 17 New Bond Street from 1859 until 1890.

This interesting Renaissance pendant, depicting a lizard with bared jaws, splayed feet and curled tail, has a pearl-hung body enameled in translucent green, a diamond-set head with redstone eyes, a line of table-cut rubies along its back and a white enamel, scaly pattern underside. It hangs from an enameled link with a pendant pearl.
Lizard pendants are high on the list of pieces produced by Spanish goldsmiths during the Renaissance era—a good example was retrieved from the Spanish Armada vessel *Girona*, which sank in 1588 off the Irish coast. This piece had an estimated value of £7,000-10,000 when it came up for auction at Christie's, London.

This stunning emerald and diamond pendant was the property of Lord Bolton, whose family traditionally held the title of Lord Lieutenant of the North Riding in Yorkshire. The superb quality of the main gem gave it an estimated value of between £50,000 and £60,000.

Far Right: This exquisite Art Deco emerald and diamond pendant, which was expected to raise $115,000 to $135,000 at auction was another of the great jewels once owned by the socialite Vera Hue-Williams.
Made in around 1925, the emerald drop with diamond cap hangs from a baguette-cut, detachable diamond panel, which in turn hangs from a large diamond collet.

Top Left: This Portuguese 18th century silver pendant—5.8cm long—was set with a cruciform pattern of cabochon emeralds at a later date.

Center Left: This gold pendant, with a domed banded agate center set with rose-diamonds, has sloping sides and a loop with red and white enamel detail and corded rims. It dates to the second half of the 19th century.

Bottom Left: This gold pendant has an amethyst center that has been carved in cameo with the profile of a woman wearing a pendant earring and a fillet in her hair. The pearl-hung frame, with open-work scroll border, is enameled in deep blue and white and there is a brooch-pin on the reverse. Made in about 1870, it is probably Austro-Hungarian.

Above: Elizabeth Claypole was the second, most favored daughter of the English soldier and statesman Oliver Cromwell. She died at the age of 28 in 1658 and is buried in Westminster Abbey. It is her portrait that has been chased on to this 18th century silver-gilt medallion, with its wreathed border and loop and ring for suspension.

SILVER

Above: This lozenge-shaped pendant, made circa 1870, displays Revivalist characteristics. The open-work *fleurs-de-lis* mount has a pearl and ruby collet center, while the border is beaded with diamonds and sapphires. The loop used to hang it from a necklace is enameled.

Although the pendant is signed by Phillips Bros., it is thought that Carlo Giuliano, who worked closely with the Phillips Bros. boutique in London prior to setting up on his own, created the design. The pendant also displays the Prince of Wales's feathers mark.

Left: This Victorian pendant has a pearl and diamond twin heart center, pearl rims and a diamond-set suspension loop.

It was sold with a lozenge-shaped brooch of similar design that is not shown in this photograph. Both pieces were made circa 1880.

Top: This 17th century miniature frame pendant, with its minute black, white, pink and turquoise enamel detail, has an almost full-face portrait on one side. The lady, in an orange dress trimmed with blue and gold, is wearing a pearl necklace and earrings. The other side has a glazed center bordered by red stone collets. Probably of Dutch origin, it was made around 1640.

Above: This gold and enamel pendant, a cabochon opal at its center and with a rose diamond-set drop, was created by Carlo and Arthur Giuliano at the turn of the century. Those lucky enough to touch a piece of Giuliano jewelry will find it heavy compared with other Victorian pieces, because the company always used solid gold.

and, thinking that she has been killed by a lion, commits suicide. Then Thisbe, who is still alive, arrives and finds Pyramus dead, so she kills herself on his sword. Shakespeare was to recreate these tragic events in *A Midsummer's Night Dream*.

Atalanta, according to Greek mythology, was nurtured by bears and grew up in the wild to be an excellent hunter. She refused to marry any man who could not beat her in a race; those who tried and lost, she killed. Eventually, when Hippomenes arrived as a potential suitor, he threw three golden apples of the Hesperides at her feet to distract her, so he won and they were married.

Made around 1650, the locket is painted in the style of the Toutin family (Jean and his son, Henri), who were well known for their painted enamel techniques.

Center: Lockets, tiny cases with hinged lids in which a memento such as a photograph or lock of hair can be kept, developed from reliquaries (jewelry in which religious relics were kept) in the Middle Ages. In the 16th century, a sovereign would give a locket with his portrait inside to courtiers. After that, lockets were used as general pieces of jewelry.

This late 17th century double hinged gold locket is delicately painted both inside and out with figures and landscapes, ruins and water. The rims and loop by which to attach it to a necklace have been enameled turquoise.

Bottom: This is an early 17th century Spanish pendant. Made with gold, enamel and rock crystal, the center is pierced with the contracted form of "Maria." While it has red, white and green enamel scrolls around the edges, the reverse supports red, green and blue enamel on a white ground.

The pendant was sold on a flattened gold chain, which is not seen in this picture.

Top: The pictures on the outside of this gold and enamel locket depict two ancient legends, that of Pyramus and Thisbe, and that of Atalanta and the golden apples of Hesperides.

The story of Pyramus and Thisbe, told by Ovid, is of two young lovers, who—kept apart by their parents—manage to communicate through a crack in the wall of their houses. When they finally agree to meet, Pyramus arrives to find the bloodstained cloak of Thisbe

Far Left: This mid-17th century gold pendant has a central ruby bordered by rectangular-cut rubies and white enamel foliage, which are surrounded by a border of translucent enamel flowers. A locket back was fitted at a later stage.

Center: This Spanish gold reliquary pendant has a gem-set front pierced with two spears flanking a cross between colored enamel scrollwork. The underside of the pendant is engraved and enameled with a cross, the letters "IHS" and three nails. It is thought that the pendant was made at the beginning of the 17th century.

The pendant once belonged to Sir Sidney Nolan, a Melbourne-born artist whose works are found in London's Tate Gallery, the Museum of Modern Art in New York and various national galleries in Australia. He died in November 1992.

Above Right: This 17th century silver gilt reliquary pendant contains carved and painted ivory figures of St John the Baptist and St Antony of Padua. The outside of the pendant is decorated with applied foliage and wirework.

Probably of Portuguese origin, the pendant was sold attached to a 19th century plaited gold mesh fob chain with a tasseled end (not visible in this photograph). A fob chain was always used to attach a pocket watch to a man's waistcoat pocket. It takes its name from the waistcoat pocket, which was known as a fob.

Left: This oval gold and enamel religious medallion has Christ painted on one side and the Virgin Mary on the other. It was sold alongside a slightly larger, but similar medallion, which had one side painted with The Annunciation, the other with the Virgin Mary, the Christ Child and St John. Both date to the second half of the 17th century.

Also in the lot was a 12cm high gold and gilt metal *chatelaine*, from which three 16th century enamel plaques, portraying St Peter, St Paul and St Joseph, hung.

71

Right: This is an unusual reliquary pendant in the shape of a cross, which used to belong to Phyllis Phillips' Collection, Phyllis Phillips being the wife of Hugh, an eminent anaesthetist at the end of the 18th and early 19th centuries.

The front of the cross is covered in gold with instruments of the Passion on blue and white enamel ground. Similarly colored black and white *fleurs-de-lis* are found on the terminals. Dating to around 1600, the cross is probably Spanish.

Below Right: On one side of this gold *verre æglomisæ* pendant is the Virgin, her hands clasped in prayer, on the other is the Angel of the Annunciation. At the top is a suspension loop so that the pendant can be hung from a chain and at the bottom is a drop pearl. Dating to the 17th century, the pendant is either of Spanish or Italian origin.

Verre æglomisæ is a method of decorating glass by applying either gold or silver leaf and engraving it with a fine needlepoint. The addition of a layer of varnish or another sheet of glass then protects the engraving. Although this technique was developed in ancient times and used by the Egyptians and Romans, it is named after Jean-Baptiste Glomy, the 18th century French writer, artist and art dealer.

Below Far Right: This pendant has a hinged rock crystal cover, which opens to reveal an oval enamel plaque painted with Christ at the Column. The beaded and simulated wirework open-work gold mount is set with garnets and seed pearls.

On the back of the pendant, the words "Munus Amoris Amor" and the *chi-rho* monogram have been engraved—*chi* and *rho* are the first two letters of the Greek name for Christ and the monogram therefore represents Him.

While the enamel plaque dates to the 18th century, the mount was made around 1880.

Right: The cover of this gold locket is engraved with the Virgin of Sorrows, a sword piercing her breast, on one side and the Paschal Lamb on the other. Inside are enameled three pink roses and a white cross hanging from a black and white checkered band, all of which are enclosed in a wreath and forget-me-not surround. The date, 1698, and owner's initials, O.H.A.M. have also been enameled on to the inside.

It is thought that the locket belonged to a German abbess and—if this is so—the distinctive black and white checks would imply that she was a member of the House of Hohenzollern, which ruled Brandenburg-Prussia from 1415 to 1918 and Imperial Germany from 1871 to 1918.

Above Left: This Victorian gold heart-shaped locket is decorated with rose diamonds and blue enamel.

Above Right: This delicate Vever pendant features a leaf spray set below a cascade of baroque pearl berries and above a baroque pearl drop. The leaf has been created from pale green *plique a jour* enamel set between delicate veining. Made around 1905, the 8.5cm tall endant has French assay marks and was sold in a fitted case bearing the address Vever, 14 Rue de la Paix, Paris. During the late 1880s, Maison Vever's designs were based on Renaissance and Oriental art. However, this family firm is best known for its Art Nouveau jewelry, which was considered second only to that of René Lalique and won many awards at international exhibitions, including the 1900 Paris World Exhibition.

Right: This necklace is a typical example of René Lalique's work. The pendant, showing two enamel figures who appear to dance among fall leaves, is framed by a diamond-set and enamel floral surround. It hangs from an enamel bar link neck chain that is barely visible in this photograph.

Made around the time of the Paris Exhibition, the pendant was sold in a fitted case inscribed Lalique, Paris.

Far Right: This is a fine example of a *Belle Époque* piece of jewelry. The enameling, in particular, is regarded as a tour de force, the warm rays of the sun blending beautifully into the blue sky.

In stark contrast, the delicate diamond work picks out an arcaded garden with festoons, fountains and a swan beneath a bridge. The tranquil scene is framed by diamond collets; the back is covered in deep blue guilloche enamel.

Made in around 1900, the pendant measures 6cm in diameter. It was expected to fetch between £10,000 and £15,000 at Christie's auction house in London.

BELLE ÉPOQUE

Above: Is it an angel? Is it an aristocrat? This very unusual Art Nouveau pendant necklace, made in about 1890, depicts a well-dressed woman with wings.

Plique a jour enamel (in various shades of green and blue), blister pearls and circular-cut diamonds have been used to create her wings and dress, while her figurehead has been made from white coral. On her head is a stylized diamond headdress.

The beautiful seed pearl latticework sautoir, on which the pendant hangs, has diamond connections. Christie's estimated its value at between £10,000 and £15,000.

ART NOUVEAU

Above: The brilliant-cut diamond in the center of this pendant weighs 4.86 carats. Its value was estimated at £10,000-15,000.

PARURES

Above: The 38cm long necklace has bow-shaped diamond links dotted with baroque pearls and three pearl-hung festoons, each one with a central table-cut emerald in a wreath border. Of similar design are the baroque pearl earrings. A baroque pearl is a natural or cultured pearl that has formed around an intrusion in the oyster, with the result that it is irregularly shaped. Although they can look impressive, a baroque pearl is worth intrinsically less than a perfect specimen.

Previous page: part of a fine sapphire and diamond suite. See page 82.

A PARURE (or suite as it is sometimes called) is a set of jewelry comprising, for example, a necklace, two bracelets, ear rings, hair ornaments, brooch and ring, which are made of the same kind of gems and are designed to be worn all at the same time. If a set of jewelry only has a few of the pieces that make up a parure, it is known as a demi-parure.

Traditionally, if a parure is made with diamonds it is destined for formal evening wear and if it contains other precious stones—usually a large colored gemstone framed by a border of small diamonds—it is meant for day wear.

Parures were important pieces of jewelry for both men and women at the beginning of the 16th century. Henry VIII had at least two, which included a broad collar, pendant and chain, dress clasps and hat pieces. There is a later mention of Madame de Pompadour (1721–64), Louis XV's mistress, having a diamond parure, but otherwise they did not come back into fashion until the early 19th century when they came strictly under the umbrella of women's jewelry.

It was Josephine, the first wife of Emperor Napoleon Bonaparte, who made parures fashionable again. She used the state jewels belonging to the former Kings of France to create a number of parures in neo-classical style. Marie-Louise, Napoleon's second wife, continued this tradition by having a parure made from 24 ancient cameos among the state jewels.

However, perhaps the most famous parure of all time was the Renaissance style "Devonshire Parure" created by the London jewelry house of C.F. Hancock in 1856. The parure was made for Countess Granville, wife of Lord Granville who headed Queen Victoria's mission to Moscow, to wear at the coronation of Tsar Alexander II. The seven-piece (coronet, diadem, bandeau, comb, stomacher, necklace and bracelet) gold parure was covered with polychrome enameling, as well as cameos and intaglios representing mythological characters and famous Romans.

Interestingly, bridal parures have been popular in Scandinavia since the 15th century, where the church or local authority is still expected to possess a set of jewelry that can be lent to a bride on the occasion of her wedding. Although once they were made from diamonds, these days they are more likely to be made from crystal. A bridal parure usually consists of a crown, necklace, brooch and earrings.

Above: This Graff demi-suite only has a necklace and ear rings. The focus of the two-row diamond collet necklace is the hexagonal-shaped sapphire in a baguette-cut diamond border from which an emerald and pear-shaped ruby pendant hangs. At the back, the necklace has only one row of collet diamonds. The ear clips mimic the pendant.

Laurence Graff founded Graff in Hatton Garden, the center of London's diamond trade, in 1960. Since its establishment, Graff has handled some of the world's most important gems, including the "Porter Rhodes," the "Windsor Diamonds" and the "Hope of Africa." It has also produced some of the most exciting and glamorous jewelry of its age. As a result, Graff is recognized as a world leader in the jewelry industry.

Right, Top and Center: This simple, yet striking, brilliant-cut diamond collet and scroll parure includes a necklace, bracelet, ring and earrings.

Above Right: This suite of Fred jewelry comprises a necklace, ear clips and ring. The necklace is made from three rows of 42cm long cultured pearls, which have two pear-shaped amethyst and pavé-set diamond foliate connections, the style of which is reflected in the ear clips and ring.

Above: This is a rare and important *giardinetti* (little garden) style demi-parure, which combines some of the most attractive features of 18th century jewelry, such as lively colors and a naturalistic design. All three pieces feature cushion-cut rubies and rectangular-cut emeralds mounted in diamond-set flower and foliage settings of silver and gold.

Not many jewels of this type have survived, so it is unusual to find them together—although ribbon slides on the back of the pendant suggest that it was once attached to a necklace. And it is difficult to know where the demi-parure was made, for while the robust silver backs of the three pieces point to an Iberian origin, the design—and some French control marks—suggest that they came from France.

The demi-parure was sold in a fitted case, along with additional safety hoops for earrings.

Above: This Art Deco suite of jewelry, made at the start of the 1930s, consists of a necklace, two bracelets, ear clips and a ring.

The front section of the necklace has two rows of graduated rectangular-cut sapphires with square and baguette-cut diamond spacers, at the center of which there is an open-work buckle panel suspending three sapphire drops. The front section is attached to the alternate sapphire and diamond single-line back chain by diamond scroll connections. The two matching bracelets are set with rectangular-cut sapphires and baguette-cut diamond two-stone spacers.

The ear clips bear some resemblance to the diamond scroll connections of the necklace, while the ring—signed by Cartier—is a very simple single-stone sapphire. As would be expected for such a fantasic set of jewelry its estimated price was very high at $75,000-105,000.

Above: Here is a classic emerald and diamond suite. Set in diamond clusters at the front of the 42cm long necklace are five oval-shaped emeralds weighing 7.18, 7.53, 8.26, 8.67 and 9.86 carats. In between the clusters are marquise and diamond collet spacers. From the central cluster hangs a 9.01 carat emerald in a diamond cluster drop. The two-row diamond neck chain has marquise and diamond collet connections.

One of the emerald and diamond double cluster ear pendants is set with emeralds weighing 7.39 and 8.20 carats, while the other is set with emeralds weighing 7.92 and 9.33 carats. The ring, of similar design, is set with an emerald weighing 6.60 carats, which is surrounded by a diamond single-line border with navette-cut diamond shoulders on a plain hoop.

The total weight of the emeralds in the suite is 89.95 carats. It was expected to reach up to £200,000 at auction at Christie's London. branch.

Right: A necklace, bracelet, ring and ear pendants make up this very ornate parure, but only the first two items feature in this photograph.

The front panel of the necklace is made of diamond foliate and collet detail, while the tapered necklace has a calibré-cut ruby spray and scrolls. The half-hoop bangle, which is very similar in design, has a central ruby and diamond panel, with applied star motifs on the hinged hoop.

GIARDINETTI

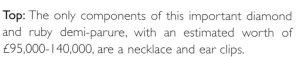

Top: The only components of this important diamond and ruby demi-parure, with an estimated worth of £95,000-140,000, are a necklace and ear clips.

From the diamond cluster necklace hang five large cabochon ruby and diamond clusters, while the ear clips—of similar design—each have a cabochon ruby, surrounded by marquise-cut diamonds.

The demi-parure was sold with certificates from the Swiss Gemmological Institute stating that two of the rubies, both of Burmese origin, have been treated with a substance that fills voids and fissures.

Above Left: This impressive, if somewhat garish, multi-colored sapphire parure from the 1950s consists of a necklace, brooch, bracelet watch and ring.

The bib necklace features yellow and blue sapphire flowers with ruby and sapphire bombæ central clusters. The gas hose bracelet watch has three sapphire cluster flowers, which open to reveal a circular dial designed by Van Cleef & Arpels. The brooch and ring are of a similar design.

Above: There are six pieces to this diamond and turquoise parure, but not all of them are visible in this photograph.

The stylized necklace has turquoise flowerhead clusters with diamond bombæ centers alternating with triple leaf connections. The bracelet is of similar design, while the three brooches have turquoise flowerheads and latticework detail.

Above: This impressive mid-19th century diamond and topaz parure, mounted in silver and gold, comprises a 47cm long pendant necklace, 16.5cm long bracelet, drop earrings and two rings. The necklace has a detachable pear-shaped pendant with diamond bow surmount, which is similar in style to the earrings, and the bracelet has a detachable cruciform cluster center. All of the pieces are presented in the original fitted and tooled red leather case bearing the retailer's name and address of Marc Garland, 23 rue du Bac, Paris.

The most sought after color of topaz is light sherry brown, not unlike the color of the gemstones in this necklace.

Top Right: A necklace, brooch, brooch pendant, two bangles and a pair of pendant earrings make up this extensive pink topaz, emerald and gold parure, which was made around 1830.

Above: There are four parts to this yellow, orange, pink and blue sapphire and diamond suite of Boucheron jewelry: a necklace, bracelet and earrings.

Frédéric Boucheron, who soon acquired a reputation as a precious stones expert, a masterful technician and a creator of beautiful jewelry designs, founded the house of Boucheron at the Palais Royale in 1858. The company remains in family hands to this day.

Above: This demi-parure consists of a sapphire, diamond and pearl sautoir and earrings. The multi-strand pearl sautoir has barrel-shaped sapphire and diamond links of latticework design, and the ear pendants of similar design are suspended from diamond collet and pearl surmounts.

Right: This spinel and diamond parure may comprise a necklace, ring and ear pendants, but only the 42.5cm long necklace, with its oval-shaped spinel and rose-cut diamond clusters and graduated spinel fringe with spinel collet spacers, is visible in this photograph.

Right: This suite is of intricate strawberry design, which —it can only be assumed because the bracelet and ring both bear the signature—were designed by Cartier.

The estimated cost of the suite, which includes a 38.5cm long necklace and 16.5cm long bracelet fashioned from cushion-cut rubies and diamonds was £30,000-40,000.

Below Far Right, Bottom: This intricate demi-parure features a bracelet, brooch, ring and earrings, all with cabochon emeralds and pave-set diamond leaves. It was made in about 1950.

Below Right: The brilliant-cut diamond collets and cabochon emeralds in the bracelet, ear clips, cuff links and ring of this Chantecler demi-parure appear to be randomly set.

Pietro Capuano, a Neapolitan nobleman whose family had been in the antique jewelry trade, founded Chantecler immediately after the Second World War in Capri. He called the shop Chantecler because it was his nickname. Popular among high society, Chantecler was known for the originality and elegance of its jewelry.

Far Right, Center: Chaumet is famous for its jewels, many of which—like this demi-parure made in about 1950—replicate nature. The rigid bark textured gold necklace is entwined with diamond detail, while the stylized strawberry is made from citrine and diamond. The matching ear clips are of similar design.

In around 1780, Etienne Nitot founded the house of Chaumet in rue St Honoré, Paris, where it soon gained the patronage of the French court. It made the crown for the imperial coronation of Napoleon, a tiara as a gift for Pope Pius VII and Empress Marie-Louise's wedding parure. The business changed hands several times before 1885, when Joseph Chaumet assumed control. For many years, the Maison Chaumet continued to create jewelry for the courts of Europe, Russia, the Near East and India.

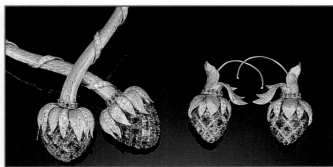

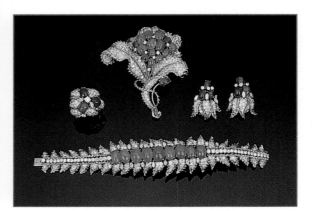

Right and Above: The necklace and bracelet of this ruby and diamond parure can be seen in the photograph—the ring and ear clips are not visible. The unusual look of these two pieces has been created by using an open-work palmette design set with diamonds and graduated cabochon rubies.

Below Far Right: This is a rare George III parure dating to circa 1810. The 56cm long necklace, with alternating rectangular-cut emeralds and cushion-shaped diamonds has a rectangular-cut emerald and diamond cluster clasp. The 19.7cm long bracelet is very similar, while the 4.1cm wide quatrefoil pendant has a huge rectangular-cut emerald.

Below Right: This necklace and bracelet were not sold together by Christie's, but are obviously matching. Both have brilliant and baguette-cut diamond graduated leaves in the center, with circular and baguette-cut diamond scroll surmounts. The pavé-set chains on both have graduated diamond collets and baguette-cut scroll intersections. They were made in around 1950.

Right: Once again, the ruby and diamond pieces grouped together here were not sold by Christie's as a parure, but they are certainly very similar and look as if they should be worn as a set.

All feature a crossover scroll design set with rectangular-cut rubies and pear-shaped diamond two-stone leaves. The necklace (estimate: £35,000-45,000), bracelet (estimate: £22,000-28,000) and watch each have a graduated baguette-cut chain, with the bracelet and watch having some extra pear-shaped diamond detail. The estimate for the ring was £4,500-6,500, while the earrings (with a flexible pear-shaped diamond tassel drop) had an estimate of £8,000-12,000. The watch, with its movement by Piaget, was expected to raise between £22,000 and £28,000.

All these pieces were created by Mouawad, which was founded in Lebanon in 1890 by David Mouawad, but really came into its own under the guidance of his grandson, Robert. Considered by many to be a creative genius, he was inspired by both Eastern and Western influences to create unique and distinctive jewelry.

89

Right: A gem-set suite of strawberry design jewelry, comprising a 42cm long necklace, 18.5cm long bracelet, ear pendants and ring, the pavé-set ruby strawberries within a pavé-set diamond necklace of scroll motif and navette-cut emerald detail, the bracelet, ring and earrings of similar design.

Below Right and Below: This romantic suite of jewelry features heart-shaped sapphires in the necklace, earrings and ring. Even the wristwatch, which is signed by De Laneau, almost has a heart-shaped face.

Below Far Right: The firm of Kutchinsky may well have made this pearl and diamond suite, because the face of the watch bears the Kutchinsky signature.

Hirsch Kutchinsky and his son Morris started making fine jewelry in East London in 1893. Thirty-seven years later, Morris's sons took over the business, which, after the war, was so successful that they opened a store in London's Knightsbridge, where it remains today.

Right: The four very pretty pieces of this parure—a necklace, bracelet and pendant earrings—all feature marquise and brilliant-cut diamonds and pear-shaped sapphires. The pear-shaped sapphire drop of the pendant earrings can be removed.

Below: This very classic parure has a 42.9cm long necklace of cabochon emeralds and brilliant-cut diamond clusters with quatrefoil diamond intersections, that perfectly matches a 17.8cm long bracelet, pendant earrings and ring.

Below Right and Far Right: Only the house of Bulgari could have created this demi-suite of ruby, diamond and hematite jewelry, so distinctive is its style.

    The 38cm long necklace is an articulated pavé-set diamond and oval-cut ruby pierced barrel-link 18 carat band with hematite (a type of iron ore) spacers; the 17cm bracelet is similar. The estimated price of the two pieces was $35,000-40,000.

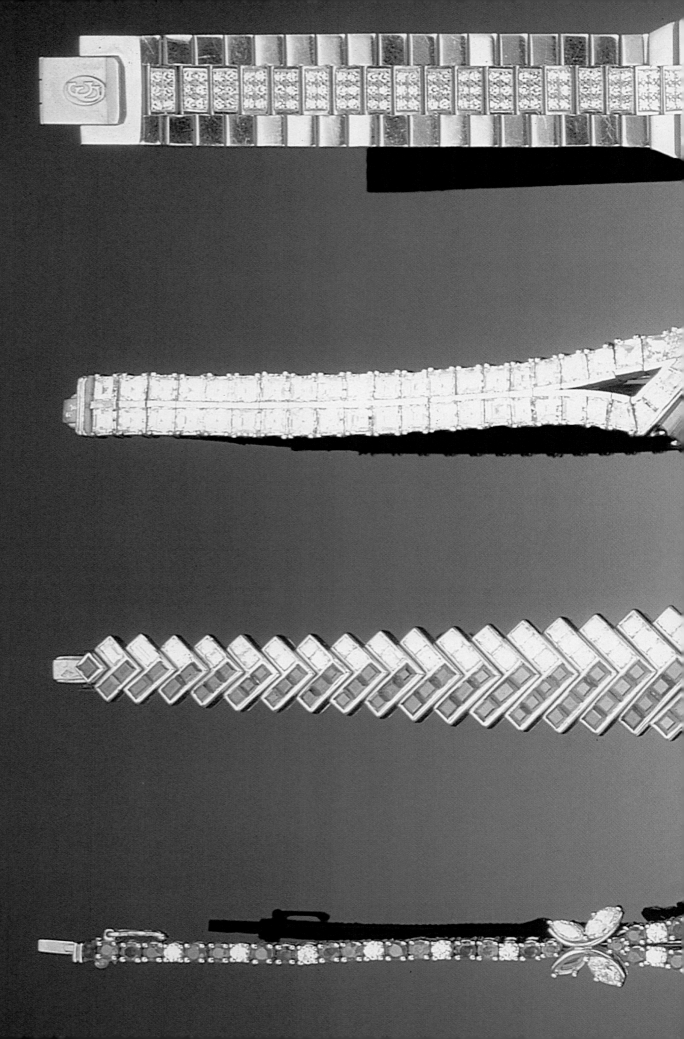

WATCHES

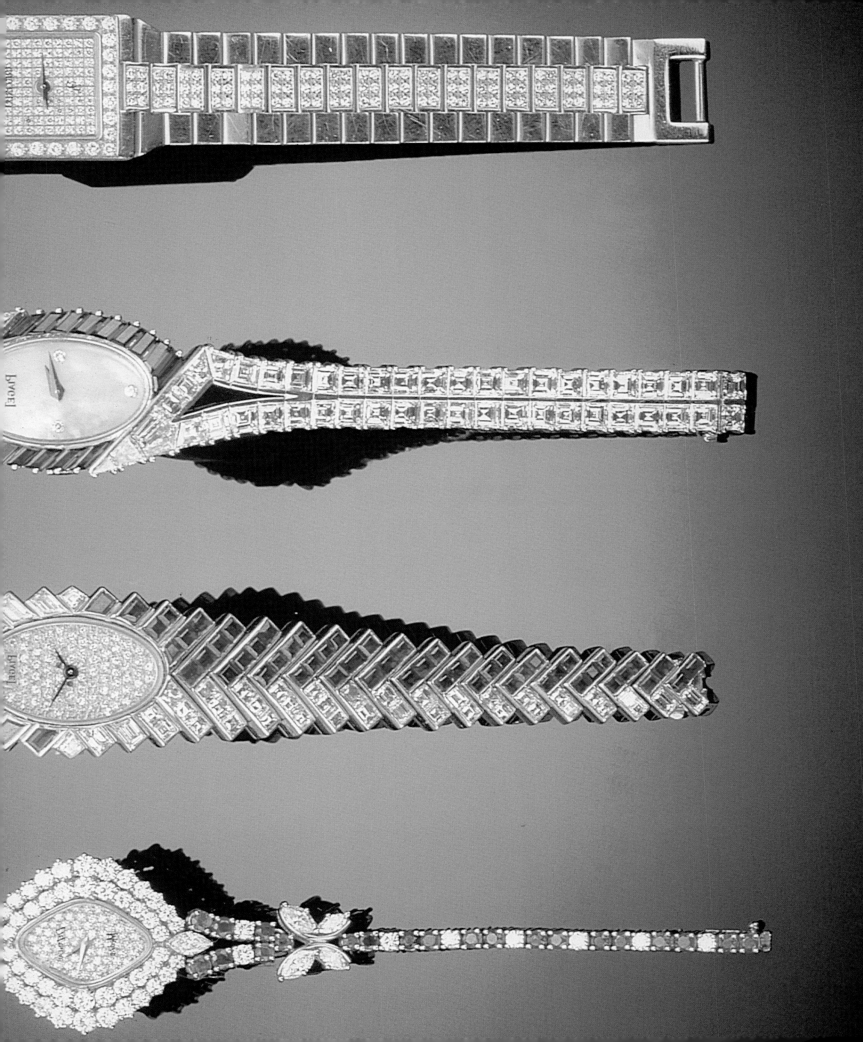

Previous pages: A selection of jeweled watches.

Above: These two lady's wristwatches were both designed by Cartier and were made within a year of each other, but they are quite different in style. One, made in 1929, has a rectangular dial on a twin line strap with a cabochon sapphire winder. The estimate on it was £2,000-3,000. The other has an unusually shaped face with a rose-cut diamond border and a seven-row pearl bracelet. It was made in 1930 and had a slightly higher estimate at £5,000-6,000.

Left: This almost galactic looking Art Deco diamond bangle watch was made by the leading French jewelry house of Van Cleef & Arpels in around 1930. The rectangular dial is flanked by pavé-set and baguette-cut diamond shoulders, which have a stylized flared adjunct.

THE FIRST WATCH, A TIMEPIECE SMALL enough to be either worn on a wrist or carried around by a person, is thought to have been made around 1500, when the invention of the mainspring made portable clocks possible.

To maintain a constant speed as the mainspring ran down, a fusæe (a cord wound round a conical barrel) was used. In recent times, of course, a small battery has replaced the mainspring as a source of energy. Another modern development has been the possibility of replacing the traditional analog display (with a face and rotating hands) by a liquid crystal display (LCD) face.

Over the years, several different kinds of watch have emerged, the most common of which is the wrist watch (worn on a wristband).

The first ever wrist watch was made in 1904 by the French jewelry house, Cartier, which made it for the aviator Alberto Santos-Dumont, who found it hard to use a fob watch while flying. The round cornered square watch can still be bought today.

Because they are practical to wear and are easy to read even when the wearer's hands are otherwise engaged, wrist watches have been the most popular type of watch since the First World War. Normally quite utilitarian in design, some have been dressed up in gold and gems to resemble jewelry.

More old-fashioned types of watch include the pocket (or fob) watch, which men used to carry in the pocket of their waistcoat; and the pendant watch, which women used to wear in the same way as a necklace pendant. A lapel watch was attached to jacket or dress lapel by either being suspended from a brooch or fixed on to the end of stud that went through the lapel buttonhole. The last type is the watch ring, which involved a watch being set in the bezel of a ring.

Most of the watches found in this chapter are of the wrist watch variety, although there are a couple of antique pocket watches.

TIMEPIECE

Above: So well camouflaged is the face on this lady's diamond dress watch that it simply looks like a plain brilliant-cut diamond six-row bracelet with twisted bar spacers at first glance. The square dial, signed by De Laneau, has pavé-set diamonds.

Right: This rare keyless hunter pocket watch appears to have been a group effort. While the finely painted enamel dial showing a Turkish harem has been signed by J. van Mergem, the thin plated bar movement is thought to be by Piguet, the movement is signed with the stamp of Edmund Jaeger and the watch is signed by Cartier. Made around 1920, the front and back covers of the watch feature multi-colored floral enamel decoration and Arabic script on a blue background.

Below Right: This ultra slim hunter dress watch, with plain front and back covers, has a gold engine-turned bezel and a matt silvered engine-turned dial with Roman numerals and blue steel moon hands. Measuring 5cm in diameter, it is signed by Cartier, while the casemaker's stamp is "EJ."

Below Far Right: The photograph shows the back of this Art Deco Egyptian revival pocket watch, with its Tutankhamun mask painted in polychrome enamel on a red guilloche enamel ground. The circular dial has both Roman and Arabic numerals, with inner 24 hour chapter rings. Made circa 1925, the dial and movement are both signed by Cartier, Paris.

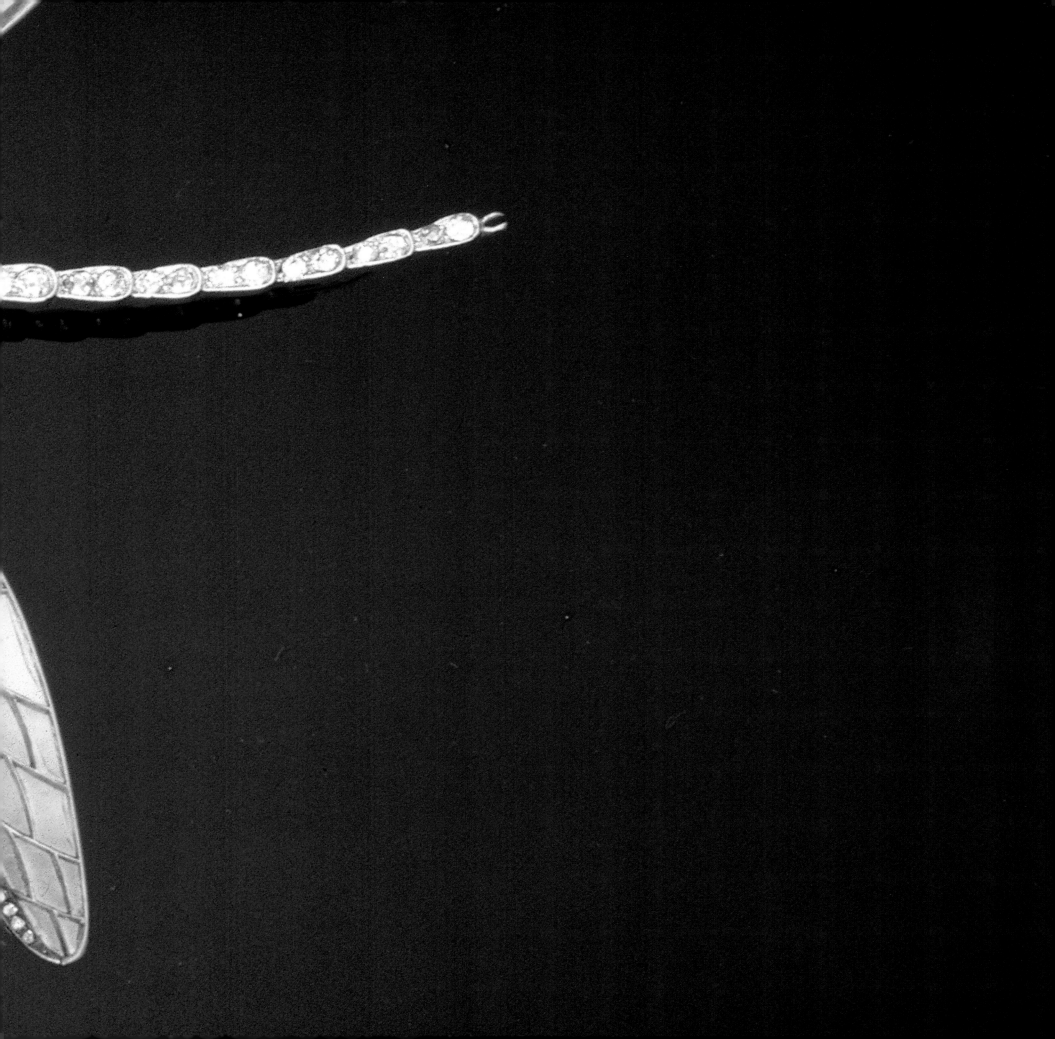

Above: Here we have three brooches, all of them very typical of the *Belle Époque* era. The top one (estimate: $ 4,000-6,000) is a diamond and yellow diamond festoon brooch, made around 1920. From the stylized lotus terminals hang a two-row collet festoon and two bell-shaped mounts with *briolette* diamond drops. The center brooch (estimate: £2,000-3,000) features three brilliant and rose-cut diamond-set arrows with calibré-cut ruby detail, which are bound together by a heart-shaped cluster and an open wreath surround. The bottom one (estimate: £6,000-8,000) also has diamond-set arrows with calibré-cut ruby details, but on this occasion they are bound by an open bow knot and a much larger wreath.

Previous pages: An Art Nouveau enamel and diamond brooch by Lacloche. See page 104.

IN ANCIENT TIMES, IT WAS KNOWN AS A fibula and functioned as a safety pin. Today, it is a brooch. However, the most important feature of this piece of jewelry is still the pin, by which the brooch can be attached to an item of clothing or a hat, either as a fastener (as in days gone by) or as decoration.

There is evidence that brooches existed in Byzantine times, if not before. Certainly, samples have been found that date to around the 4th or 5th century—Germanic jewelry was always both functional and decorative, so brooches were high on the priority list. And because they were functional, they were worn by both men and women.

In the 10th and 11th centuries, brooches were important pieces of jewelry, used either to fasten clothes or, sewn into a garment, for decorative purposes. By the 13th century, brooches were the most frequently worn piece of jewelry and would remain so right up until the end of the 19th century.

In the late 17th century, Brandenburg, a long horizontal brooch with tapering ends, became fashionable, first as a man's jewelry item, then as a woman's. In the early part of the century, brooches tended to be very simple, with more emphasis on the gemstone rather than the setting.

In the last quarter of the 19th century, as the public's interest in natural history rose, it was very fashionable for creatures from the insect, reptilian and animal world to be reproduced in jewelry form. Some of the most popular brooches were of dragonflies, butterflies, bees, spiders, owls, swallows, frogs and lizards. Often worn in multiples, these small brooches were scattered all over a woman's bodice. They were also worn on the shoulder or pinned to a belt or hat.

The Art Nouveau movement at the end of the 19th century changed the style of the brooch completely. Out went heavy gold settings and gems. In came graceful free flowing lines depicting floral patterns, insects and female bodies, created from enamel, with cabochon gem highlights.

This style was replaced, at the start of the 20th century, by the pretty garland, wreath and bow-and-swag style of the Edwardian era.

However, the greatest brooch innovation in many centuries came in the 1930s, when the double clip—a versatile piece of jewelry used on less formal occasions—was introduced. The two clips could either be worn together as one large brooch or separated and worn as a matching pair.

Moreover, although they looked like normal brooches, they differed in that they had either a hinged support that fastened onto the edge of a garment or a hinged double prong that could be passed through fabric, rather than a fastening pin.

Other slightly unusual types of brooch include the stomacher, a large brooch (some with removable pendant drops) worn on the bodice of a dress, which ceased to be popular towards the end of the 19th century. Bar brooches, horizontal by design, have gemstones or decorative motifs along their length. A ring brooch is made from a complete circle, to the back of which is a hinged pin slightly longer than the diameter of the circle.

These days, brooches are not as popular as other items of jewelry and men, among whom they were popular in years gone by, have stopped wearing them.

Left, Above and Below: The geometric Art Deco brooches on this page contrast strongly with the more floral styles of the *Belle Époque*. All were made around 1925–30. The one in the large photograph to the left is a brilliant-cut diamond panel brooch and carried an estimate of £5,000-6,000. The pair of Cartier rectangular clips (top, left) feature brilliant and baguette-cut diamonds with black enamel detail. They were sold with a bangle attachment with an estimate of £6,000-8,000. The brooch in the center of the top row, a stylized geometric shield made from brilliant and baguette-cut diamonds, had an estimate of £700-900. The final one (top, right), a diamond and calibré-cut onyx panel brooch of stylized palmette design, has a diamond collet two-stone drop and was made circa 1925. In the Christie's catalog, it had an estimate of £6,000-8,000.

Below: A Victorian rose-diamond and sapphire bee brooch.

Above, from left to right

These two cruciform brooches are similar, having both been made around the turn of the century.

The first, with an estimate of £800-1,200, is set with pearls and small diamonds, while its foliate terminals are enameled in translucent orange and opaque white scrolls. The back bears the initials A.P. which probably refers to the jeweler Alfred Phillips, although there were a number of jewelers with the initials A.P. in operation at this time.

The second (estimate: £400-500) has translucent green enamel pearl-set terminals in a *fleur-de-lis* form with white enamel scrolls. The back also has the initials of A.P. although they are rather indistinct.

An attractive diamond pierced panel brooch, the shaped rectangular panel decorated with diamond leaves and collets on a pierced lattice-work background. Estimate: £1,200-1,500

A pearl and diamond bar brooch, designed in a series of three bows with articulated festoons and a central pear-shaped diamond and single pearl-drop each from a diamond collet line. As can be seen in the photo, a bar brooch is a decorated horizontal brooch.

Right: This rather mischievous looking frog is made from pavé-set diamonds, with a calibré-cut sapphire and emerald stripes, plus cabochon sapphire eyes.

By way of explanation, pavé-set refers to the setting, which could be likened to paving stones in that many small gemstones are set very close together so as to cover the entire piece and conceal the metal base. In order that the gems fit together snugly, calibré-cut diamonds, which are small and oblong or elliptical in shape, are used.

Above, Left: The bar of this brooch is entwined with serpents, created with the use of scaly black enamel. Above the heads of the snakes are rose diamond-set wings and, at the top, a coral bead finial. It was made by Carlo Giuliano in the late 19th century.

Above, Right: The focus of this 4.5cm wide gold bar brooch, with its five floral drops, is the central flower-head. Dotted with pearls and coral beads, it was made around 1860.

Center, Left: This brooch represents Mercury with a winged caduceus standing on a calibré-cut sapphire globe, which is flanked by calibré-cut emerald wreaths.

Center, Right: This 3.5cm wide queen's bodyguard of Scotland badge brooch is decorated with diamonds and enamel.

Right: The center of this 19th century coral brooch features a small carved dog with crossed paws and turquoise-set collar. The wirework surround has four carved rosettes.

Far Right: This carved opal maple leaf has a single diamond collet (which—if you screw up your eyes tightly—could almost be a raindrop) and a diamond-set stem.

Right: This small circular brooch, with a translucent red enamel center at the heart of which is a diamond, has a pierced border set with rose diamonds. Made by Carlo Giuliano, it dates to the late 19th century.

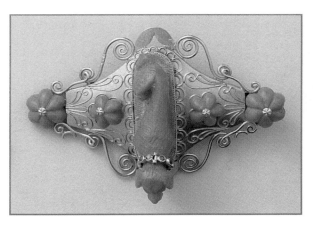

On this page, we have three excellent examples of Art Nouveau jewelry.

Right: The female face framed by an elaborate dark green enamel headdress that has been decorated with marguerites was created by the great master of the Art Nouveau age, René Lalique, in around 1900. From the bottom of the headers hangs a baroque pearl. It is all the more valuable (it was estimated at £8,000-10,000) for being signed by Lalique and sold in its original fitted case.

Far Right: This stunning orchid brooch, which is mounted in silver and gold, was made by Tiffany circa 1890. The white and yellow enamel orchid, with brown enamel spots, rose-cut diamond detail and diamond-set stem, is so realistic you could almost pop it in a vase of water.

Below Right: Here is another Lalique brooch, this one featuring the head of a nymph in profile, with gold husks superimposed on sweeping tresses of green enamel hair. Made around the turn of the century, it, too, is signed by Lalique and was sold in its original fitted case.

102

Right and Above: Here are two diamond and turquoise leaf brooches, estimated by Christie's in London at £10,000-12,000 apiece.

Below, Far Right: This is a Tiffany brooch with a graduated textured scroll set with brilliant-cut diamonds and cabochon emeralds border.
Estimate: £3,000-5,000

Below Right: This is a very unusual looking brooch, which looks as though it is mimicking a firework. At its center is an octagonal-cut ruby, from which alternating brilliant and baguette-cut diamond flexible tassels fall. Four of the tassels suspend oval-shaped rubies.

Below: This extravagant looking brooch is made from a centrally set cabochon sapphire surrounded by a cushion-shaped sapphire triple cluster, highlighted by tiny diamond collets.

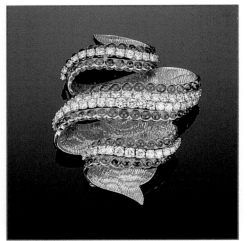

103

Right: Dragonflies were often used in Art Nouveau jewelry, because—as can be seen in this example—their wings were suited to the use of *plique-a-jour* enamel.

Aside from the polychrome *plique-a-jour* enamel wings, this dragonfly is endowed with rose-cut diamonds on its wing tips and a diamond-set body and tail.

Made around the turn of the century and measuring 12cm wide, the dragonfly was made by the jewelry house of Lacloche. The Christie's estimate for this piece was £8,500-9,500.

Below, Far Right: This brooch, made circa 1910, has a circular-cut diamond at its center. The open-work calibré-cut emerald and rose-cut diamond surround is littered with emerald collet details.

Below Right: Here is another classic piece of Art Nouveau jewelry. The vision of a polychrome *plique-a-jour* enamel girl holding a peacock feather was set within a swirling line of diamonds, by the designer Louis Aucoc, who made this piece around 1900.

Aucoc (1850–1932) was known for employing floral and linear motifs in simple forms. He often collaborated with the designer G. Landois and figurative representations were cast from models by the sculptor Edmond Henri Becker, who also worked for Boucheron.

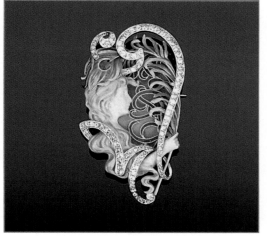

Right: This Art Deco brooch, made circa 1925, resembles a basket of flowers. The turquoise vase, with its black enamel surround and diamond base, is filled with carved turquoise flowers that have black enamel stems. Further color is added by ruby, emerald and multi-colored diamond collet details.

Above Center: This 6.7cm high George III cruciform brooch has a central cushion-cut diamond cluster, four oval-shaped clusters to the cardinal points and collet and scroll intersections and terminals. Mounted in silver and gold, it was made circa 1830.

Above, Far Right: This brooch features a cushion-shaped sapphire set in two tiers of brilliant-cut diamonds.

Right: This is an amazing intense yellow diamond flower clip brooch. Made by Cartier in 1953, the diamond in the center of the flower weighs 102.07 carats. An accompanying certificate from the Gemmological Institute of America states that the diamond is a natural fancy intense yellow and has Vs2 clarity.

The magic figure of 100 carats is rarely surpassed in the world of diamonds and so when one does appear in a Christie's sale, it generates great excitement. The "Ashberg" was a very similar stone to this one. A fancy yellow color, it weighed 102 carats and was once mounted in a magnificent Kokoshinik tiara that was said to form part of the Russian Crown Jewels. Remounted by the Swedish jewelers Bolin as a pendant, it was sold at Christie's in Geneva for $804,000 in May 1981.

However, the Ashberg was a yellow amber color, which would indicate a tint of brown, whereas this stone is fancy intense yellow and displays a quite remarkable purity of color and clarity (Vs2), especially given its size.

Such a jewel would have to have been mounted by a top jeweler such as Cartier, which has shown a deftness of touch in creating this brooch. The balance is superb, while the movement created in the petals and the angle at which the stone is inclined, combine to produce a remarkable brooch. Unsurprisingly the estimated sale price was phenomenally high at $670,000-790,000.

Right: The central feature of this antique brooch is a cushion-shaped sapphire, which has a foiled back in a closed setting. The use of foil was popular up until the end of the 19th century—this brooch was made around 1870—because it enhanced the coloring and brilliance of certain gems.

Aside from the sapphire, the brooch has several rows of rose-cut and cushion-cut diamonds, and diamond collet and scroll terminals with knife-edge and collet graduated pendant drops. It was sold with both ring and brooch fittings.

Below: This Frohmann abstract cluster brooch is set with brilliant and marquise-cut diamonds, dotted with cushion-shaped rubies. Made in the mid-1960s, it measures 5.8cm wide.

Above: The lion in René Boivin's gem-set clip brooch looks as docile as a cat lying by a winter's log fire. The pavé set yellow diamond articulated body has a baguette-cut ruby, sapphire and emerald mane, and emerald eyes. Mounted in 18 carat gold, it has French assay marks. It was estimated that it would fetch $30,000-40,000.

Left: This unusual-looking Cartier brooch has three cabochon emeralds with a central diamond cluster and a diamond scroll surround.

Above: This Harry Winston brooch, which Christie's estimated at $350,000-450,000, is set with a 34.45-carat cushion-shaped sapphire in a pear-shaped and marquise-cut diamond cluster surround. It is mounted in platinum.

Right: Carvin created this really beautiful work of art. Two flamingos, their bodies made from circular, marquise and pear-shaped pink diamonds and demantoid garnets, their beaks with faceted black diamonds and their eyes with cabochon rubies, wade in a buff-top-cut demantoid garnet marsh. The two, a mother and her child, can be divided and worn separately. Mounted in platinum and 18 carat white gold, the total weight of the pink diamonds is approximately 48 carats. The cost was expected to be in the region of $450,000-550,000.

Above: This stick pinshas an opal set in a rose-diamond border with a short pearl-set chain.

Previous pages: An antique diamond jabot pin by Boucheron. See page 113.

A PIN IS A THIN, STRAIGHT, POINTED object with a head that is either used functionally to fasten down a piece of clothing or ornamentally just like any other piece of jewelry. Usually made of metal, pins can be of gold, silver, brass or iron; the head, however, may be decorated with a gem or gemstones, or an enameled or engraved motif.

Pins are, in effect, a much simpler version of the brooch, most of them designed to be worn by men.

The most common type of pin is the tie (or stick) pin, which was created to keep a man's tie in place. In the 18th century, it was made with zigzag grooving to keep stop the pin coming out of place. In the 19th century, a few twists two-thirds of the way up the pin served the same purpose. Sometimes pins were made in pairs, joined by a chain so that they could not be lost.

It was Beau Brummell (1778–1840), a close friend of the Prince Regent (later George IV), who—along with his fellow Regency dandies—started the trend for wearing cravats and neckcloths with simple, dark clothing. The only acceptable way to keep these neck pieces in place was with a tie pin.

In the 18th century, tie pins were quite simple in design, although they did start to reflect the neo-classical design that was popular toward the end of the 1700s. Following general jewelry trends, tie pins in the early 19th century were topped with cameos and intaglios. Towards the end of the 1800s, sporting jewelry was the craze and pins featured horses, foxes, tennis rackets and golf clubs. The first part of this century saw a return to much simpler styles. These days, antique tie pins are more likely to be seen decorating a woman's lapel, than securing a man's tie.

A jabot pin is similar to a tie pin. The main difference is that it is used to pin down a jabot (the ruffle worn by men on the front of their shirts and women on the front of their dresses) rather than a tie.

A surêté pin is a tie pin with a safety mechanism (in the form of a device that slips over the pointed end of the pin and is screwed on or secured by an interior spring) to keep it from being lost.

Other types of pin, while not featured in this book, include the stock pin, hat pin and hair pin. A stock pin is similar to a jabot pin in that it is used to keep a stock (a close-fitting band worn around the neck) in place, rather than a jabot.

Hat pins and hair pins were both used by women. Hat pins were used to secure a woman's hat from Victorian times up until around 1940. Similar to a tie pin in design, having a thin, straight pin and ornamental head, it was usually much longer. Hair pins, used for fastening and decorating a woman's hair, tend to be much blunter than any of the other kinds of pin and have a much longer history, examples having been found that date back to the 3rd century.

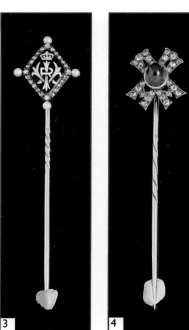
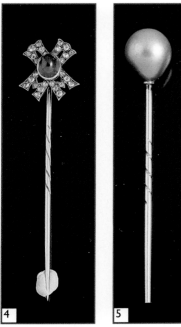
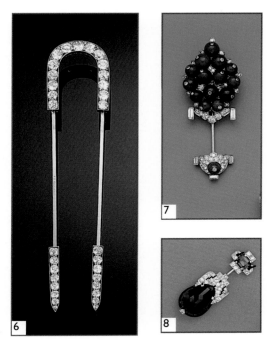

1: This is a royal presentation stick pin, having been given by Princess Louise Caroline Alberta (1848–1939), the sixth child of Queen Victoria, to Lord Colin Campbell, on her marriage to his elder brother John Campbell, 9th Duke of Argyll, on March 21, 1871.

Set in gold, the horseshoe terminal has graduated turquoise and an inner border of seed-pearls. The reverse is engraved with the following message: "Princess Louise to Ld. C on wedding 1871."

2: This 9.8cm long Italian gold stick pin is very much in the revivalist style, featuring Cupid riding on a lovebird. Embellished with granulation and applied wirework, it was designed by Giacinto Melillo (1845–1915), in the late 19th century.

The following stick pins used to belong to Lady Patricia Ramsay, the younger daughter of TRH The Duke and Duchess of Connaught and Strathearn, who—on her marriage to Admiral the Hon Sir Alexander Ramsay, in 1919—renounced (with Royal permission) the style and title of HRH and Princess, and adopted that of "Lady."

3: And in the third lot was a black and white enamel royal cipher stick pin with a rose-diamond border and pearl terminals.

4: In the second lot was a single cabochon sapphire and rose-diamond royal "AA" monogram stick pin.

5: The first lot comprised three single pearl stick pins that were all alike, they were all very simple like the one in the photograph with its single pear-shaped black pearl terminal.

6: This very elegant antique jabot pin was created by the house of Boucheron in around 1880. The horseshoe-shaped pin, mounted in both gold and silver, is set with cushion-cut diamonds and has cushion-cut diamond detachable terminals.

7: This is a very stylized Art Deco surêté pin, using lapis lazuli and brilliant and baguette-cut diamonds to depict a 5.6cm high fruit tree.

Lapis lazuli is usually a deep blue color, but sometimes has mottlings of white. Because it is opaque, it is cut either *en cabochon* or flat, but never faceted. In ancient times, it was thought that lapis lazuli provided protection against a snake bite.

8: The decorative part of this Art Deco surêté pin, which is signed by Cartier, has a pear-shaped emerald faceted bead set in a diamond geometric mount with a black enamel border. At the other end of the pin is an emerald and diamond stylized terminal with black enamel open circles.

CAMEOS

Previous pages and Above: The picture on this Roman sardonyx cameo, which was made in the 1st century BC, shows a helmeted warrior restraining a horse with one hand, while holding a shield embossed with a Medusa head in the other. The 17th century gold frame has an inner ropework border that is picked out in green and pink enamel on a white ground.

The cameo has an interesting provenance, having belonged to both Sir Charles Newton-Robinson and Sir Robert Mond.

Sir Charles, who was born in October 1853, was a barrister, Chairman of the Council of Land Union and member of the British épée team at the 1906 Olympic Games, but he was also an amateur collector of engraved gems who wrote several books, including *Description of Engraved Gems in Burlington Club's Greek Exhibition*, an event at which this cameo was displayed.

Sir Robert was a well-known researcher of pure and applied chemistry, electro-chemistry and color photography, who helped his father discover new carbonyls, but he shared Sir Charles's passion for old engraved gems.

TRADITIONALLY, A CAMEO IS A HARD-stone, such as sardonyx, which has different colored layers. One layer, in the case of sardonyx it is the white layer, is carved away in relief to reveal the underlying layer, so that the relief design and background contrast with each other.

Cameos are probably the oldest form of jewelry known to man. Two-colored carved stones (used as seals) have been found that date to the Sumerian era—the Sumerians lived in Mesopotamia from the 4th millennium BC until the 20th century BC. The first cameos, however, date from the Hellenistic period in the 2nd century BC.

Cameos continued to be made right through the Roman and Byzantine eras, but really came into their own during the Renaissance, when princely patrons such as Lorenzo de Medici commissioned lots of cameos from Italian master jewelers. They have remained popular pieces of jewelry ever since, being made into brooches, pendants and finger rings.

Cameos were a major part of the neo-classical style in the 18th century. By this stage, cheaper versions were being made from Bilston enamel medallions that were painted with classical heads, and ceramic and glass imitation cameos.

From the 1770s, Josiah Wedgwood molded stoneware, the surface colored with metallic oxides of which cobalt blue is the most common, and decorated it in relief with white.

In 1804, Napoleon chose cameos to decorate his coronation crown and, the following year, set up a school of gem engraving to encourage the art. Napoleon's obsession with cameos was due to their links with the Greek and Roman Empires that he himself hoped to emulate.

Not only he, but his wives had pieces of jewelry made from cameos. His first wife Josephine had a tiara cut from a large shell, which was subsequently carved with mythological scenes and mounted in gold. His second wife, Marie Louise, had a parure made with 24 ancient cameos from the French royal collection. So fashionable was the cameo at the time that one French magazine suggested cameos should be worn on belts, necklaces, bracelets and tiaras.

As the 19th century wore on, cameos became even more popular and cheap varieties were bought as souvenirs on the continent—shell cameos came from Sicily, while lava cameos could be bought from Pompeii.

From the start of the 20th century, however, cameo making fell into decline.

Cameos are not only of importance to the jewelry world, the early pieces in particular are of historic significance because the carved scenes often reveal contemporary customs, philosophies and important events. However, this is not so true of the 19th century, when most cameos showed decorative female portraits, often inspired by Queen Victoria or the actress Sarah Bernhardt.

There are several very famous cameos in existence, two of them being the "Epsom Cameo" and the "Noah Cameo."

The "Epsom Cameo," so called because it was found in Epsom in Surrey, is an irregularly shaped cameo made from a garnet, with a gold, late 7th century Anglo-Saxon surround. The carving shows a bearded man wearing a Phrygian cap.

The "Noah Cameo," carved from onyx, depicts a scene from Noah's Ark. Its origin is uncertain, but there are indications that it was made in the first half of the 13th century. Having said that, the gold frame in which it is mounted is characteristic of French metal work dating to the 14th and 15th centuries, and the words "LAVR MED"—the mark of Lorenzo de Medici—are engraved on the doors of the ark.

Above: A picture of a reclining Silenus hailing a small satyr adorns this small oval sardonyx cameo which dates to somewhere between the 1st century BC and the 1st century AD. The gold mount is much more recent, dating to the 19th century.

Above: This necklace is mounted *en esclavage*, which literally translates as "in slavery." It is a term to describe necklaces such as this that feature more than one chain —the style was particularly popular in Normandy in the mid-18th century.

The seven onyx cameos depict the heads of gargoyles, which date to the 17th or 18th century. Some time later, probably in the second half of the 19th century, each cameo was embellished with a rose-cut diamond and set in an applied gold wirework mount.

Right: This cameo was created around the beginning of the 19th century. Made from gray agate with a gold frame of beaded rims, it features the head of Germanicus (15BC–19AD), son of Drusus and Antonia and husband of Agrippina, in profile.

Below Right: This example dates to the 16th century. Made from sardonyx, it is engraved with a triumphal procession. Close inspection reveals Venus holding an arrow to her heart as she rides in a lion-drawn chariot, while Cupid holds a Victory wreath above her head. In front of the chariot are musicians, with Pan playing his pipes at the rear. The 18th century border is chased with colored gold foliage and a ribbon bow cresting.

117

Above: A pair of exquisite *Belle Époque* emerald and diamond earrings, each cupola tassel drop suspended from a rectangular-cut emerald and diamond foliate mount and rectangular cluster top.

Previous pages: a pair of large, diamond encrusted, hoop earrings. See page 122.

EARRINGS HAVE BEEN WORN SINCE time immemorial. Some involve a thin hoop passing through a hole pierced in the ear lobe, while others are clipped or screwed on to the ear lobe. They can be made from any metal, be it gold, silver, platinum or gilt, and come in a wide variety of shapes, styles and sizes.

When the Sumerian Queen Pu-abi was found in her tomb, which dates to 2500BC, she had been laid to rest wearing large, crescent-shaped earrings. In ancient Egypt, earrings arrived relatively late, in 1600BC, when they were only worn by women. Two hundred years later, men had started wearing them too.

Early Hellenistic pieces were either boat-shaped with a fringe of beads or a twisting piece of gold decorated with the head of an animal. The Etruscans had two types of earring: a stud with a disc front and attachment at the back (similar to today's butterfly) and a baule earring that incorporated a little box in which perfume or a charm could be kept.

The Romans created cluster earrings and large gold dome earrings, which remained popular through to the Byzantine era, along with long pendants of cascading gems and flat crescent shapes, both of which hung from an arc of gold wire.

Following several centuries of being out of favor, earrings enjoyed something of a revival during the Renaissance, when shorter hair cuts led both sexes to wear them. The trend at the time was for pear-shaped gem or pearl drops, or fun dolphins, mermaids and blackamoors, which hung from pierced ears via a gold loop or were tied to the ear by a piece of ribbon.

In the early 17th century, geometric, rather than figurative, styles made popular earrings. Also fashionable were earstrings, made from fine silk that was attached to a hoop in the ear and hung down to the shoulder at the bottom of which would be a small pendant.

Later that century, the trend was for elaborate *girandoles*, named after contemporary candelabra, which had three crystal pendant drops attached to a bow or knot.

Earrings from the early 19th century tend to be simple, with the emphasis on the gemstones rather than the mount. After 1840, earrings became much more sumptuous and looked heavy due to their stamped out gold settings, which were hollow and therefore made them quite light. In the 1860s, novelty earrings, with steam engines or birds sitting on nests, appeared and by the end of the century, women were wearing no earrings or very simple solitaire studs.

The Art Nouveau era witnessed a decline in earrings, as brooches and pendants became more dominant. Edwardian examples were simple and elegant, with delicate platinum settings in stark contrast to the Art Deco age when bobbed hair led women to wear long, prominent earrings.

In the 1930s and 1940s, chunky gold jewelry, known as cocktail jewelry, was popular. Innovative clip fittings, an alternative to the traditional pierced and screw attachments, revolutionized earrings. The result was more compact pieces, with decoration concentrated around the lobe, although it sometimes followed the curve of the ear upward. Often, because earrings framed the face, they were set with the best stones.

After the Second World War, pendant and cluster shapes were all the rage and the clip fitting was widely used because of the trend towards heavier settings. The designs of the 1950s through to the present day are very varied and follow no particular pattern.

Above: A pair of brilliant-cut diamond loop earrings.

Right: A pair of diamond and baguette diamond scroll design ear clips, of knotted spray design.

Far Right: A pair of amethyst and diamond pendant earrings.

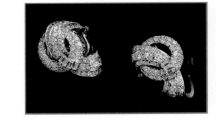

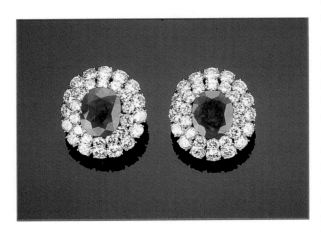

Below Left: Each of these Van Cleef & Arpels ear clips is set with a cushion-shaped ruby—one weighs 7.74 carats, the other 6.15 carats—surrounded by two rows of brilliant-cut diamonds.

They were sold with two certificates. The one from The Gübelin Gemmological Laboratory states that both the rubies are of Burmese origin, while the other, from The Precious Stone Laboratory, states that the stones are from Mogok (in Burma) and that there is no evidence of heat treatment.

Traditionally, the best rubies in the world have come from Mogok in Burma. The history of the Mogok mines is long and complex—Stone Age tools have been found on the site providing proof of antiquity. The mines, in an area of thick jungle, took three weeks to reach from the capital of Rangoon at the beginning of the 20th century. On the last day, because the mines lay more than a day's journey from the nearest village, visitors were forced to camp out, hence the name

Mogok, from *mochok*, the Burmese word for "nightfall camping ground."

Up until the 19th century, the Burmese King controlled the mines, but when the British won the second Anglo-Burmese war (1852–53), they seized the gem-bearing zone and set up Burma Ruby Mines Limited. However, due to difficult access to the mines and poor management, the company was liquidated in 1931. The mines were subsequently returned to the Burmese, who resorted to age-old extraction methods, the most prevalent of which was open-cast mining. Two or three men would operate a pit, roughly 4 meters deep and 20 meters wide. As soon as they found byon (gem-bearing gravel), the removal of the rubies would begin. In 1962, when General Ne Win took control of Burma through a military coup, the mines were nationalized and mining at Mogok is now restricted.

These two beautiful earrings were valued by Christie's, London at between £100,000 and £150,000.

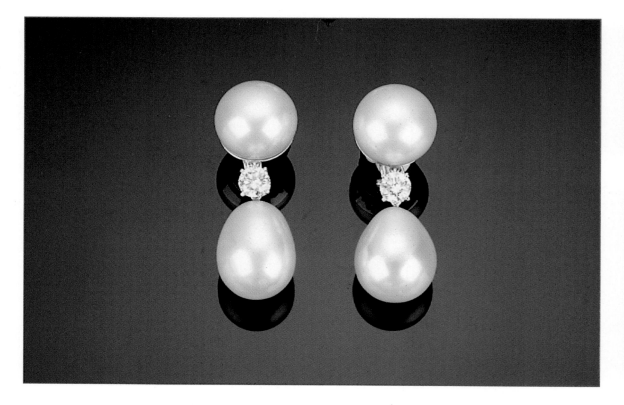

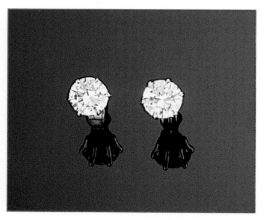

Above: Here is a rare pair of South Sea cultured pearl and diamond ear pendants—the pearl surmounts measuring 17.21mm and 17.20mm in diameter, while the cultured pearl drops measure 20.23mm and 20.09mm in diameter. The estimate was just as large at £25,000-35,000.

Top Right: These ear clips are set with brilliant-cut diamonds. Earrings such as these—with a hoop—are known as Creole earrings and were worn from the mid-19th century.

Above Right: These ear studs are set with brilliant-cut diamonds, one weighing 1.01 carats, the other 1.00 carats. An accompanying certificate from The European Gemmological Laboratory states that both are "D" color and internally flawless—about as perfect as white diamonds can be.

Right: These long ear pendants, made in about 1925, are typical of the Art Deco style. From cultured pearl tops hang two rows of diamonds, which—in turn—suspend a cultured pearl drop with a pavé-set diamond cupola surmount.

Above: Each of these Cartier ear pendants has a drop-shaped gray pearl with a diamond surmount, suspended from a stylized wing surmount that is set with brilliant and baguette-cut diamonds. Signed by Cartier, they were made circa 1930.

A certificate from The Gem Testing Laboratory of Great Britain confirms that both the pearls are natural.

Top Right: Each of these ear clips has five pavé-set diamond petals, oval-shaped ruby stamens and a central diamond collet.

Above Right: These Victorian drop earrings each feature an oval-shaped ruby surrounded by diamonds, with a diamond collet top. Mounted in silver and gold, they were made in about 1880.

Above Right: Each of these ear pendants has a pear-shaped emerald and diamond cluster, which is attached to a circular-cut emerald and diamond cluster surmount by a marquise and diamond collet line. They were made circa 1920.

123

124

Both pairs of ear clips above were created by the great American jewelry house of Harry Winston—Gwyneth Paltrow wore won of his necklaces when she picked up the 1999 Oscar for best actress.

Left: The focus of the first pair of ear clips is a brilliant-cut diamond, from which pear-shaped diamonds and rubies emanate in a double scroll surround.

Above: Each of the second pair of platinum mounted ear clips is set with a pear-shaped sapphire (one weighs 11.88, the other weight 12.10 carats) in a marquise-cut and pear-shaped diamond cluster surround. The estimate for this pair was $75,000-95,000.

Right: These extraordinary-looking Art Deco ear pendants have an octagonal-cut sapphire (one weighing 7.75, the second weighting 8.68 carats), which is surrounded by a pierced triangular panel set with calibré-cut sapphires and circular and baguette-cut diamonds. The flexible tassels are made from calibré-cut sapphires, baguette and circular-cut diamonds.

The Gübelin Gemmological Laboratory has examined the gems and confirmed that the sapphires are from Kashmir and show no evidence of thermal treatment. This testamony from a respected scientific institution is the main reason why the pendants were given an estimate of $75,000-92,000.

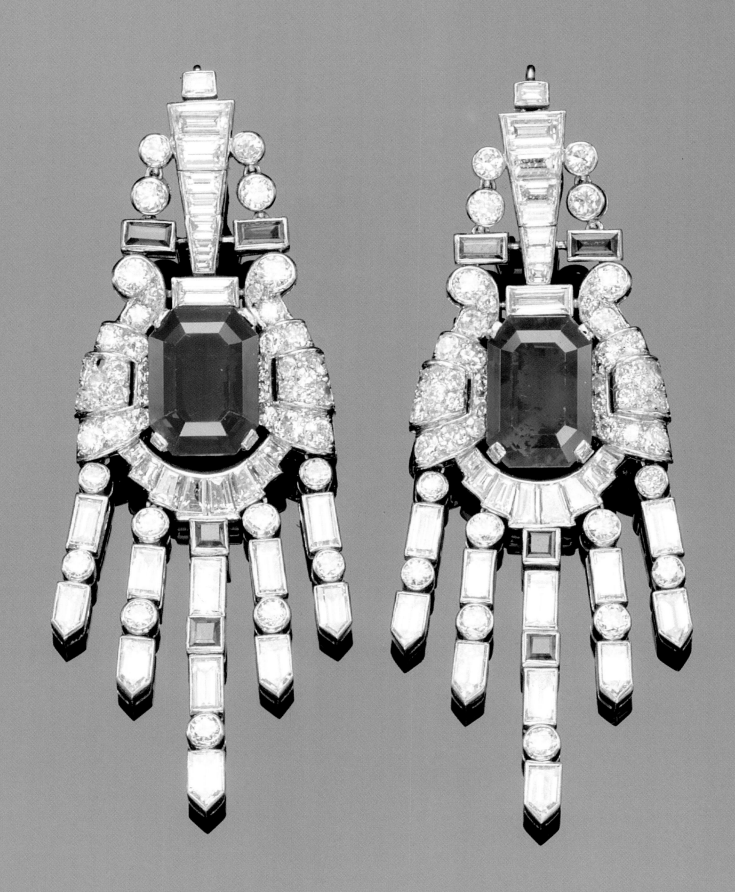

HEADDRESSES

Above: This elegant head ornament is made from a series of intertwined brilliant and baguette-cut diamond flowerheads and scrolls, at the center of which is a brilliant and square-cut diamond spray.

The spray and both ends of the head ornament are detachable, forming a clip brooch and a pair of earrings respectively.

Above Right and Previous pages: Here is a really impressive Austro-Hungarian tiara—the kind of jewelry that every little girl grows up dreaming she will one day wear. The tiara is made from five graduated *fleurs-de-lis*, each one set with pearls and other gems in black and white settings that have red, blue and green details. Along the base is a band of small diamonds in pyramidal settings.

In style, the tiara is very close to the lily diadem made for the Royal House of Bulgaria by Kochert of Vienna about 1889. From that and other head ornament designs, it is likely that Kochert made this tiara in the 1880s.

THERE ARE SEVERAL TYPES OF HEAD-dress, including diadems, *bandeaux, ferroniere* and tiaras.

Diadems, worn around the brow of a man or woman, have been in use from ancient times. Made of metal, often gold, they resembled a wreath and were often decorated with gemstones and pearls.

The Egyptian pharaohs and their wives wore diadems, and one was found in Tutankhamun's tomb. Made of gold, it has a detachable front piece which is made in the form of the head of a vulture and the body of a cobra. It was made to symbolize the unification of Lower and Upper Egypt in around 3100BC.

Greek diadems, made from either gold or silver, could be simple or decorated with motifs, filigree work and granulated gold. Roman diadems progressed from wreaths of leaves to headdresses that anticipated the royal crown.

Diadems existed in Europe in the Middle Ages, but in the form of a chaplet, which was worn by unmarried girls and was the predecessor of the bridal crown.

The *bandeau*, a narrow band that encircled the forehead, appeared to take over from where the diadem left off. It was worn by Italian women in medieval times and then in western Europe from the mid-19th century until the early part of this century.

The *bandeau* was not dissimilar from the *ferroniere*, a band worn around a woman's forehead with a gem in its center. Originally worn in Italy in the 15th century, when they consisted of a silk or velvet ribbon knotted at the back of the head, they came back into fashion in the 19th century as a fine gold chain or string of beads. Some even had pendants hanging down at the temples.

The term tiara was used to describe the headdresses of the ancient Persians. At the end of the 19th century, tiaras were an essential part of court and society dress in Europe and America. Only worn by married women, they made popular wedding presents. They were still an integral part of court society right up until the outbreak of the Second World War.

Although tiaras come in many different shapes, sizes and degrees of ornamentation, they are generally made from a curved, vertical band that has a central peak, heavily encrusted with jewels. Tiaras that rise to a point in the center are known in England as Spartan diadems—they were particularly popular in the 1790s and early 1800s.

In Victorian times, necklace tiaras were fashionable. Composed of a series of jeweled ornaments, each had a tiny hook that could be attached to a tiny ring on the adjacent ornament, so that all the ornaments could be brought together into a vertical position to create a tiara. Other necklace tiaras could be attached to a wire frame, thus converting it into a tiara.

Also, in reverse, some tiaras could be converted into brooches for use on less formal occasions.

Above: This is a pretty necklace tiara. Five open scroll and foliate panels, each with two diamond collets (one in the center, one as a pendant) alternate with scroll intersections, while the back chain is made from open scrolls. The necklace was sold with three tiara and one comb fittings. The estimate given by Christie's in London was £60,000-80,000.

Overleaf: This is a delicate, very modern-looking tiara. The main lattice band is set with diamond collets and unusual star panels. At the top, 12 old-cut diamond terminals and six larger second row diamonds weigh a total of 75.30 carats, while the central cushion-shaped diamond weighs 24.08 carats. This is another piece that was of such high value that Christie's did not publish an estimate.

Top: These baton-style cufflinks have ruby bead terminals.

Above: These Tiffany cufflinks depict the zodiac sign of Leo, one bearing the head of a lion, the other that of a lioness.

Right: Simple, but elegant, these Cartier cuff-links have a circular onyx face and diamond-set borders.

Previous page: Cufflinks once belonging to King George V of England. See opposite page.

134

CUFFLINKS ARE A TEMPORARY WAY OF fastening the cuff of a shirt. Unlike cuffs that have been buttoned up, the cuffs of a shirt that have been fastened by cufflinks do not overlap, the cufflinks having been threaded through two buttonholes.

Cuff links are, along with tie pins, one of the few pieces of jewelry worn by men and, as a result, they are often highly decorative or humorous. In recent years, they have also become popular with women.

Cufflinks are usually made of gold, silver or another metal, although silk cufflinks are also popular these days. They come in many styles and shapes, some set with gems, others with enameled or engraved metal. And while most are identical pairs, some just have harmonious designs.

Victorian cuff links were often made with gold, and were more decorative and ornate than modern ones. As with tie pins, animals of sporting significance were popular cufflink motifs. In Edwardian times, as was the trend, cufflinks were very simple.

There are several ways in which cufflinks work. Some have a short, loose link chain connecting the back with the front; others have a back joined to the front by a fixed bar. Then there are those with a fixed bar to the head that have a swivel bar that slides through the buttonholes and is twisted into a secure horizontal position. Finally, there are those that have two separate pieces, a front with an extension that snaps into a back with a depression. The latter is sometimes known as a press stud.

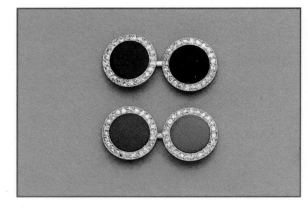

The following two sets of cufflinks have royal connections.

Above: The first pair were given to Commander Harold Campbell, CVO, DSO, RN, Groom of the Robes by King George VI soon after his coronation, as they are accompanied by a letter that reads: "I send you these links as a souvenir of my Coronation when you attended me as my Groom of the Robes. George RI. 1937."

Made primarily from onyx, each face has a rose-cut diamond and enamel royal cipher "GR" in its center. They were sold in the original fitted leather case bearing the royal monogram of "GVIR."

Right: The second pair were given by King George V, when he was still Prince of Wales, to the physician Dr. Thomas Clarke. He gave them to his nephew, who then gave them to his son, on both occasions as a 21st birthday present.

The four oval faces of the cufflinks are engraved with the Prince of Wales's feathers, coronet and motto "Ich Dien." Made in around 1905, they were sold in a fitted case bearing the retailer's address of Elkington & Co. Ltd., Glasgow.

Above: This very rare collection of antique table-cut diamonds weighing 8.51, 8.09, 7.70, 5.19 and 4.71 carats was estimated at £90,000-110,000.

Previous pages: Part of a selection of 17 loose gemstones. See opposite page.

138

THE CUT AND CARAT OF A GEMSTONE **are important in assessing the value of any stone, be it a diamond, ruby, emerald or sapphire.**

The most common cuts are brilliant, eight, rose, step, cushion, emerald, cabochon, square, baguette, marquise (navette), heart-shaped, trapeze and calibré. However, none of them is actually cut —cutting is a misnomer as the facets are ground onto the stone.

The brilliant cut made its first appearance in the late 17th century. With 58 facets (the table and 32 facets above the girdle, 24 facets below), it is generally recognized as the best way to set off a diamond because it allows as much light as possible to be reflected from the bottom of the stone up through the top.

The eight cut, developed in 1910, is a modern version of the brilliant cut, but with less facets, and, therefore, is used for small diamonds of 0.5 carats or less.

The rose cut took over in the mid-17th century from the table cut. Used mainly for diamonds, it has 24 facets and a flat bottom, so less material is lost than in a brilliant cut.

The step cut tends to be used for large colored stones, such as sapphires and emeralds.

The cushion cut is often used for sapphires and rubies.

The emerald cut, confusingly, is not just used on emeralds—it is used on large transparent gemstones including diamonds, topaz and aquamarine. Developed in the 19th century, it only became popular in the 20th century.

The cabochon cut, in use since the 19th century, does not involve faceting and is often used on heavily flawed stones that would not benefit from faceting.

The square cut featured very heavily in the Art Deco age.

The baguette cut—the shape of the French bread stick—is often used in conjunction with other types of cut.

The marquise cut, an elliptical modification of the brilliant, was popular in the 18th century, fell out of favor in the 1800s, and found favor again in the modern era.

The heart-shape cut was discovered in the 18th century, became popular in the Edwardian era and is once again finding favor these days—Sophie Rhys-Jones's engagement ring to Prince Edward included a heart-shaped diamond.

The trapeze cut, first used regularly in the 1920s, is still sometimes used for large stones.

A calibré cut does not refer to a particular cut, but to stones that have been cut into a shape to fit a particular setting. Using any kind of faceting, they tend to be small.

The term "carat" comes from the Greek word *kiration*, which describes the fruit of the carob. Perhaps not surprisingly, therefore, a carat is related to the carob seed, which has an average weight of about 0.2 grams. Today's metric carat, the standard unit of weight used today in jewelry for gems, weighs exactly that, one-fifth of a gram. This world standard was accepted at the beginning of the 20th century. Carat is, of course, also used to describe the quality of gold, 24 carats representing the purest kind of gold.

It is important to remember that although diamonds are generally the most valuable of all the precious stones, at the top level of purity and perfection, both rubies and—on the odd occasion—emeralds are more valuable, on a per carat basis, because they are more rare.

These two sets of gemstones belonged to Basil William Anderson (1901–1984), one of the world's leading gemmologists for 60 years and one of the greatest pioneers of this specialized science.

Above Left: A collection of 17 gemstones (zircon, chrysoberyl, morganite, beryl, yellow orthoclase, feldspar, citrine, zircon, tanzanite, sinhalite, fluorite, zircon, topaz, tourmaline, tourmaline, kunzite, spinel and blue topaz).

Above: A collection of nine gemstones (pyrope garnet, kunzite, aquamarine, yellow/green beryl, orthoclase feldspar, phenakite, topaz, scapolite, white topaz).

1: A brilliant-cut diamond weighing 1.37 carats.
Estimate: £2,000-2,500

2: A cut-cornered rectangular diamond weighing 2.99 carats.
Estimate: £3,000-3,500

3: A brilliant-cut diamond weighing 2.70 carats.
Estimate: £3,500-4,000

4: A brilliant-cut diamond weighing 2.75 carats.
Estimate: £3,500-4,000

5: A brilliant-cut diamond weighing 2.48 carats.
Estimate: £6,000-8,000

6: A cushion-shaped ruby weighing 1.58 carats.
Estimate: £2,000-3,000

7: A cushion-shaped red spinel weighing 4.96 carats.
Estimate: £1,000-1,500

8: A cut-cornered rectangular topaz weighing 31.85 carats.
Estimate: £2,000-2,500

9: A cushion-shaped sapphire weighing 6.25 carats.
Estimate: £2,500-3,500

10: A brilliant-cut fancy yellow diamond single-stone ring with a plain hoop which is not visible.
Estimate: £5,000-7,000

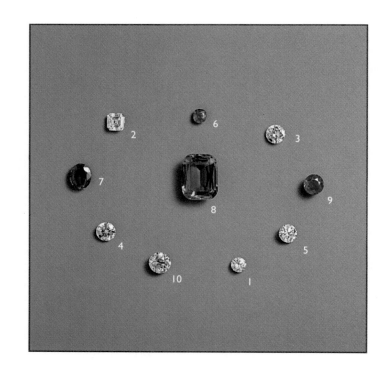

Right: In 1928, Sir Sultan Mohamed Shah Aga Khan III, the head of the Ismailian sect of Muslims, gave Cartier in Paris 38 round stones and three pear-shaped diamonds of 40, 38 and 35 carats to sell on his behalf. The French jewelry firm set them in a spectacular necklace of geometric design that was exhibited in Cairo, Alexandria and Barcelona, but—despite creating a sensation wherever it was displayed—it failed to find a buyer due to the cost involved. It was even taken on the Orient Express to Belgrade, so that it could be offered to Queen Marie, but as Yugoslavia was on the verge of civil war, her mind was on other matters. So, on the eve of the Wall Street crash, in 1929, it was broken up.

The King of Nepal purchased the round stones. Cartier kept the 35 carat stone, while the 38 carat and the 40 carat diamonds were returned to the Aga Khan. The larger stone was attached to a necklace that he gave to his son, Prince Aly Khan, and the other was re-cut into the present stone which appears here and weights 33.13 carats. It comes with a certificate from the Gemmological Institute of America stating that the diamond is "E" color (in other words, colorless) and internally flawless. A stone of this caliber is difficult to value as it is a rarity, accordingly Christie's did not publish an estimate.

Far Right: This is a truly magnificent heart-shaped diamond, with an accompanying certificate from the Gemmological Institute of America stating that the diamond is "D" colour and internally flawless, weighing 101.31 carats.

Prior to its sale, the largest diamond of this caliber that Christie's had sold weighed 62.42 carats. The price that could be expected for such a stone would be astronomical.

142

The publisher wishes to thank Christie's Images for their assistance in supplying all the photography for this book.

Right: This ring features the famous "Victory" diamond, which weighs 31.35 carats.